iPad®

PORTABLE GENIUS
FOURTH EDITION

Paul McFedries

WILEY

About the Author

Paul McFedries is a full-time technical writer. Paul has been authoring technical books since 1991 and has nearly 100 books to his credit. Paul's books have sold more than four million copies worldwide. These books include the Wiley titles *Windows 10 Portable Genius*; *iPhone Portable Genius, Sixth Edition*; *Teach Yourself VISUALLY Windows 10, Third Edition*; and *G Suite for Dummies*. You can visit Paul on the web at www.paulmcfedries.com or on Twitter at www.twitter.com/paulmcf.

Acknowledgments

Being a technical writer is an awesome vocation: You get to work at home, you get to set your own schedule, and you get to help other people understand and use technology, which is a big warm-fuzzy-feeling generator. But perhaps the best part of technical writing is getting to be among the first to not only use but also really *dive into* the latest and greatest software and hardware. The hardware side is often the most fun, because it means you get to play with gadgets, and that's a gadget geek's definition of a dream job. So, to say I had a blast researching and writing about the latest version of the iPad redefines the word *understatement*. What self-respecting gadget guy wouldn't have a perma-grin while poking and prodding this device to see just what it can do?

And what self-respecting technical writer wouldn't be constantly shaking his head in admiration while working with the amazing editorial team at Wiley? The people I worked with directly included Associate Publisher Jim Minatel, Project Editors Maureen and Scott Tullis, Copy Editor Kim Wimpsett, and Content Refinement Specialist Barath Kumar Rajasekaran. My heartfelt thanks to all of you for your outstanding work on this project.

Contents

chapter 1

How Do Get Started with My iPad?   2

chapter 2

How Do I Connect to a Network?   20

chapter 3

How Do I Configure My iPad? 36

chapter 4

How Can I Get More Out of
Web Surfing? 56

chapter 5

How Do I Make the Most of Email?   80

chapter 6

How Can I Have Fun with Photos?   94

chapter 7

How Can I Create Video on My iPad?   112

chapter 8

How Do I Manage My Contacts? 134

chapter 9

How Do I Track My Events and Appointments? 150

Introduction

There are many reasons for the success of the iPad, as well as its smaller cousin, the iPhone. However, if you polled fans of these devices, I bet one reason would quickly bubble up to the top spot: the touch interface. It's slick, elegant, and just so easy: a tap here, a tap there, and away you go.

Using the iPad touch interface is like playing in one of those seaside areas where the water is only a couple of feet deep no matter where you go; you can still have all kinds of fun, but you never have to swim hard, and there's little chance of drowning. However, if you walk out far enough in many of those ocean areas, you suddenly come to the edge of an underwater shelf, where the sandy bottom gives way to the inky ocean depths.

Your tablet, too, has its unexplored depths: hidden settings, obscure features, out-of-the-way preferences, and little-known techniques. The usefulness of some of these features is debatable, at best, but many of them can help you work faster, more easily, and more efficiently. Rather than swimming blindly through the murky waters of your tablet's deep end, what you need is a companion that can guide you through these waters, enable you to be more productive, and help you solve problems wherever you and your tablet happen to be hanging out.

Welcome to *iPad*® *Portable Genius, Fourth Edition*. This book is your guide to all things iPad packaged in an easy-to-use, easy-to-access, and eminently portable format. In this book, I cover how to get more out of your iPad by accessing all of the really powerful and timesaving features that aren't obvious at a casual glance. I also explain how to avoid the tablet's occasional annoying character traits and, in those cases where such behavior can't be avoided, how to work around it.

Finally, this book tells you how to prevent iPad problems from occurring and, just in case your preventative measures are for naught, how to fix many common problems yourself. This edition also includes updates on the new features of the latest iPads, as well as the most important and useful new features in iOS 14.

This book is for iPad users who know the basics but want to take their education to a higher level. It's a book for people who want to be more productive, more efficient, more creative, and more self-sufficient (at least as far as their tablet goes). It's a book for people who use their iPad every day but would like to incorporate it into more of their day-to-day activities. It's a book I had a blast writing, so I think it's a book you'll enjoy reading.

How Do Get Started with My iPad?

We live in a world where "design" is shorthand for "the more bells and whistles the better." That's why, when you take a look at most tablet devices, they're positively *bristling* with buttons, ports, switches, keys, and other operable knickknacks. Ah, but now take a look at your iPad, which, by contrast, has just a few physical buttons (especially the iPad Pro). That minimalist design is a sight for sore eyes in today's world, but it leads to a question: If the iPad has just a few operable buttons, how are you supposed to operate the darn thing? It's a great question, and this chapter provides the answer by giving you a big-picture tour of your iPad. You learn what those buttons are there for, and you learn perhaps the most important iPad skill: how to use the remarkable touchscreen.

Using the Top Button

Your iPad doesn't have many buttons, but it does have a few, and arguably the most important of these is the Top button (also called the Sleep/Wake button). As I point out in Figure 1.1, the Top button resides on the top right edge of your tablet, assuming you're holding the tablet in the so- called *portrait* orientation demonstrated in Figure 1.1.

1.1 On all recent iPads, you can find the Top button on the right side of the top edge.

The Top button has three main functions: sleeping and waking the iPad, powering the tablet on and off, and authorizing purchases made with the device. The next three sections provide the details.

4

Sleeping and waking the iPad

You put your iPad into sleep mode (sometimes called standby mode) by pressing the Top button. Sleep mode turns off the screen (which conserves battery power and prevents accidental screen taps), but some background activities still occur (such as receiving messages and playing music). Press the Top button once again to wake up your iPad and see the Lock screen. You now have two ways to proceed:

- Slide a finger up from the bottom of the screen.
- Press the Home button (if your iPad has one).

This either unlocks the tablet right away or prompts you to enter your passcode, if you use one (if you don't, you should; see Chapter 11).

Turning the iPad off and back on again

You won't turn off your iPad often, but here are a couple of scenarios where shutting down your tablet can be useful:

- If your iPad's battery level is critically low and you can't charge it, turning off your iPad is a good idea because then the device consumes no power. You can then turn the iPad back on whenever you need to use it.

- If a glitch has caused your iPad to freeze or behave erratically, turning the device off and then back on can often solve the problem (I talk more about this in Chapter 11).

To turn off your iPad, use one of the following techniques, depending on your iPad model:

- **Your iPad has Face ID.** Press and hold the Top button and one of the Volume buttons for a couple of seconds.

- **Your iPad has a Home button.** Press and hold the Top button for a couple of seconds.

The Slide to Power Off slider appears on the screen, as shown in Figure 1.2. (Note that you can tap Cancel if you change your mind and decide to leave your iPad on, or just do nothing and iPadOS will cancel the screen for you automatically after about 30 seconds). To shut down the iPad, use a finger to drag Slide to Power Off all the way to the right.

Note

iPadOS is the software that controls just about everything that happens behind the scenes of your iPad. The "OS" part stands for *operating system*, so in that sense iPadOS performs essentially the same functions as Windows does on a PC and macOS does on a Macintosh computer.

1.2 Use the Slide to Power Off screen to shut down your iPad.

To turn your iPad back on, press and hold the Top button until the Apple logo appears on the screen.

Making a purchase

If your iPad supports Face ID (see Chapter 11 to learn more), you can also use the Top button to authorize purchases on the device:

- **Using Apple Pay in a store.** Double-press the Top button to use your default Apple Pay credit card. To learn how to set up Apple Pay, see Chapter 3.

- **Confirming an app or in-app purchase.** When you see the Double Click to Pay message on your iPad (see Figure 1.3), double-press the Top button to approve the purchase.

1.3 Double-press the Top button to authorize an app or in-app purchase.

Using the Home Button

If you have an iPad that comes with a Home button — that is, the circular button on the face of the tablet at the bottom — then you'll use that button a lot because the Home button has quite a few functions. Here are the main ones:

- When the iPad is in sleep mode, pressing the Home button wakes the device and displays the lock screen.

- When the iPad is running, pressing the Home button returns the device to the Home screen.

- Pressing and holding the Home button invokes Siri, which enables you to control many iPad features using voice commands. (If Siri is turned off, pressing and holding the Home button opens a window that asks if you want to turn on Siri.)

7

● Double-pressing the Home button displays the multitasking screen, which enables you to quickly switch between your running apps.

If your tablet is in sleep mode, press the Home button to display the Lock screen. (This screen appears for up to about six seconds; if you don't do anything, the tablet drops back into sleep mode.)

Setting the Volume

The buttons that enable you to control the volume are located on the right edge of the iPad when you hold the tablet in portrait orientation; see Figure 1.1. There are two volume buttons:

● **Volume Up.** This is the button situated closer to the top edge of the iPad. Pressing this button increases the volume.

● **Volume Down.** This is the button situated just below Volume Up. Pressing this button decreases the volume.

When you press a volume button, iPadOS displays a horizontal volume meter that shows you the current volume level.

Working with the Touchscreen

If you've only ever controlled devices by using a keyboard and mouse, you're in for a treat when you start using the iPad's touchscreen. The "touch" part of the name means that you do everything on the iPad — zooming in and out, scrolling through screens and lists, dragging items here and there, and even typing messages — by using a finger (or, in some cases, two or more fingers) to perform particular movements, known as *gestures*, directly on the screen.

There's a learning curve, but it's not a steep one, and it won't be long before you're wishing that *every* digital device came with a touchscreen.

Note

The touchscreen is a marvel, but if you intend to do serious work on your iPad, then you might consider augmenting your tablet with some extra technology that can make your life easier. If you write a lot, then easily the most important accessory you can invest in is an external keyboard (such as Apple's Magic Keyboard or Smart Keyboard). For drawing or writing notes, consider a digital pen (such as the Apple Pencil).

Understanding touchscreen gestures

Learning to use the iPad's touchscreen means learning how to use gestures to make the iPad do your bidding. You might think there must be dozens of gestures to master, but happily there are a mere half dozen:

- **Tap.** Use a finger (it doesn't matter which one; even a thumb will work) to lightly and quickly press and release a specific part of the iPad screen. Tapping initiates just about any action on the iPad. For example, you tap to launch an app, select a check box, turn a switch on or off, enter text using the on-screen keyboard, run a command button, and much more.

- **Long press.** Place a finger on a screen object (such as a Home screen icon) for a few seconds. In most cases, long pressing an object displays a list of commands that you can perform with the object.

- **Double-tap.** Use a finger to tap a specific part of the screen twice, one right after the other. Most of the time, double-tapping something zooms in on it, and a second double-tap zooms back out.

- **Swipe.** Place a finger on the screen and then move it along the screen (which, depending on what you're doing, could be up, down, left, right, or diagonally). You use this gesture — which is also called a *flick* — to scroll through screens or lists, drag objects to different parts of the screen, and much more.

- **Spread.** Place two fingers on the screen relatively close together and then move them apart. You use this gesture to zoom in on items such as photos and web pages.

- **Pinch.** Place two fingers on the screen relatively far apart and then move them closer together. You use this gesture to zoom out of something (so it's the opposite of the spread gesture).

Searching for stuff on your iPad

Each new generation of the iPad bumps up the space available for storage: from 4GB in the original tablet to 1TB (terabyte, or 1,024GB) in a top-of-the-line iPad Pro. That's a lot of data, but the more photos, videos, music, email, messages, apps, and documents you stuff into your iPad, the harder it gets to find what you're looking for. Fortunately, your iPad comes with a powerful search feature that makes it easy to find what you want. Here's how it works:

1. **Return to any Home screen.**

2. **Swipe down anywhere on the screen.** Actually, don't swipe down from the top of the screen because that gesture displays the Notification Center instead of the Search box.

3. **Tap inside the Search box and then enter your search text.** Your iPad immediately begins displaying items that match your text as you type, as shown in Figure 1.4.

4. **Tap Search to display a list of all the results.** If you see what you're looking for, tap it.

1.4 Flick down on the Home screen and then type your search text.

Genius

If you're getting way too many search results, you can customize iPad searching to not include results from certain apps or their content. Open the Settings app and then tap Siri & Search. In the Siri & Search settings that appear, for each app you want to remove from your search results, tap the app, tap the Show App in Search switch to Off, and then tap the Show Content in Search switch to Off.

Switching from one app to another

You're free to run multiple apps at the same time on your iPad. However, it's a rare iPad user who runs apps one after the other without having to return to a previous app. For example, you might open Mail to check your messages, run a few other apps, then sometime later want to return to Mail to see if there's anything new.

That's no problem, but the technique you use to switch from one app to another depends on what kind of iPad you have:

- For all iPad models, slide a finger up from the bottom edge of the screen; stop when you get to about the middle of the screen.

- If your iPad has a Home button, double-press the Home button.

Either way, iPadOS displays the multitasking screen, which offers thumbnail versions of the apps you've used recently. Swipe sideways to bring the thumbnail of the app you want into view and then tap the app to switch to it.

Shutting down an app

The apps on your iPad don't come with a "Close" command or button. That's because when you switch to a different app, iPadOS automatically suspends the app you were working on, so you almost never have to worry about closing an app. However, there are two exceptions to this:

- Shutting down one or more apps can make it easier to navigate the app thumbnails in the multitasking screen.

- If an app is frozen and is preventing you from working in other apps, shutting down the stuck app usually fixes things.

To shut down an app that you've used recently, follow these steps:

1. **Display the multitasking screen:**

   - Slide a finger up from the bottom edge of the screen; then pause about halfway up.

   - Double-press the Home button (if your iPad has one).

2. **Locate the thumbnail for the app you want to shut down.**

3. **Drag the app thumbnail up to the top of the screen.** iPadOS shuts down the app.

Typing on the touchscreen keyboard

Your iPad comes with a touch keyboard — the portrait mode version of the keyboard is shown in Figure 1.5. To get the keyboard on-screen, tap inside any control that requires text input, such as a text box, a search box, or an address bar. You "type" on the keyboard by tapping each key, just like you would on a physical keyboard.

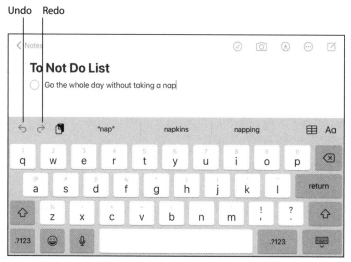

1.5 iPadOS displays the touchscreen keyboard automatically when you tap inside a text control.

Accessing special keys

Besides the usual letters, numbers, and symbols, the touchscreen keyboard offers some special techniques and keys that allow you to do some tricks:

- **Shift.** These keys — there's one to the left of the Z key and one to the right of the period (.) key — work similarly to Shift on a regular keyboard. You have two ways to use Shift on your iPad:

  - **Enter a single uppercase letter.** Tap Shift to change the letter keys to their uppercase versions and then tap the letter. The keyboard automatically returns the letters to their lowercase versions.

  - **Enter multiple uppercase letters.** Double-tap the Shift key. Again, the letters change to uppercase, but now you can tap as many letters as you need. When you're ready to return to the lowercase letters, tap the Shift key once again.

- **Key flicks.** If you take a close look at the keyboard in Figure 1.5, you see faint symbols above the regular letters: a 1 above Q, an @ above A, a % above Z, and so on. You enter one of these extra symbols using a gesture called a *key flick*: that is, flick down on a key and instead of the key's regular letter, you get the symbol above it. For example, flick down on the A key to enter an @ symbol.

Note

If you don't see the extra symbols, it means the key flicks feature is turned off. Open the Settings app, tap General, tap Keyboard, and then tap the Key Flicks switch to On.

- **.?123.** Switches to the numeric keyboard, which includes not only the numbers, but also many punctuation marks. The key changes to ABC, and you tap ABC to return to the original keyboard.

- **#+=.** This key appears when you switch to the numeric keyboard, and tapping it switches to yet another keyboard that offers even more punctuation marks and symbols.

- **Backspace.** This key appears to the right of the P key, and tapping it deletes a single character to the left of the insertion point. However, you can also tap and hold this key to delete multiple characters.

Caution

If you hold the Backspace key long enough, it starts deleting entire words instead of single characters. This really speeds up the deletion, but if you're not careful, you can end up deleting much more than you intended to.

- **Return.** Much like the Return (or Enter) key on a physical keyboard, your iPad's Return key starts a new line when you're entering multiline text, and it initiates an action in a dialog or form. However, unlike a physical keyboard, your iPad's Return key often changes its name or its function, depending on what task you're currently doing. For example, I showed earlier (see Figure 1.4) that the Return key changes to the Search key when you invoke your iPad's Search screen.

Working with predictive typing

While you're typing, iPadOS constantly makes predictions either about the word you're currently typing or about the next word you might want to enter. iPadOS displays these suggestions in a bar just above the keyboard. This is known as *predictive typing*, and iPadOS uses it in a couple of different ways.

First, predictive typing kicks in when iPadOS detects what it believes to be a misspelled word. iPadOS selects the allegedly misspelled text and then offers predicted suggestions. You have three ways to deal with these suggestions:

- To accept the default suggested word (the highlighted one in the middle), tap it, or tap the spacebar or any punctuation key.

- To use a different suggested word, tap it.

- To use your word as is (if, for example, you know it's not a misspelling), tap the suggestion that appears in quotation marks.

Second, predictive typing kicks in as you're typing when iPadOS tries to guess what your next word might be. For example, if you type *text*, followed by a space, iPadOS suggests (among others) "me" for your next word. If one of the suggestions is the word you want, tap the suggestion to enter it.

Editing with Your iPad

Can your iPad take the place of your desktop or notebook computer? It depends on what you use your computer for. If you're just surfing the web, working with emails and texts, and posting to social media, then, sure, your iPad can do all that and more. If you use your computer for more serious pursuits, then it's unlikely your iPad is up to the challenge of being your full-time computing device. However, your iPad is getting closer all the time, and as you see in the next few sections, the iPad's ever-improving editing skills sure makes your iPad a useful tool, especially when you're away from your computer.

Editing text

If you notice a typo or missing text, you might be tempted to hold down Backspace until you delete text back to the spot where you want to make your edits and then retype what you just deleted. Well, sure, you *could* do it that way, but a better and more efficient method is to move the insertion point back to the error and *then* delete the mistake or insert the text, leaving your correct typing intact.

Whether you want to fix a typo or insert new text, follow these steps to perform the edit:

1. **Press and hold on the text you want to edit.** iPadOS adds an insertion point cursor within the text.

2. **Slide your finger along the text toward the point where the typo appears.** As you slide your finger, the cursor moves along with it.

3. **When the cursor is immediately to the right of where you want to begin your edits, remove your finger.**

4. **Make your changes to the text.**

5. **(Optional) Tap at the end of the existing text to resume your text entry.**

Selecting, copying, and pasting text

Your iPad has options for selecting, cutting, copying, and pasting text. However, which of these features is available depends on whether the text you're working with is editable:

- **Noneditable text.** This type of text (for example, the text you see on a web page) can't be edited, and therefore it can't be cut. However, it can still be selected, copied, and pasted:

  1. **Tap and hold anywhere inside the text.** After a second or two, your iPad selects the text and displays blue selection handles around it, as shown in Figure 1.6.

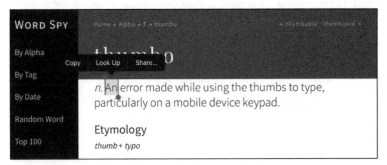

1.6 For noneditable text, select it and then tap Copy to copy it.

2. **If necessary, tap and drag the selection handles to select more or less of the text.**

3. **Tap Copy.**

4. **If you want to paste the text into a different app, open that app.**

5. **Position the cursor where you want the text to appear.**

6. **Tap the cursor and then tap Paste.** iPadOS inserts the copied text.

● **Editable text.** This type of text (for example, the text in a note, an email message you're writing, or a text box) can be edited; therefore, it can be cut or copied and then pasted:

1. **Tap and hold anywhere inside the text.** After a short pause, your iPad displays a several buttons above the text, as shown in Figure 1.7.

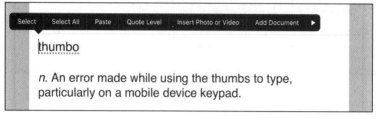

1.7 Tap and hold editable text to see these options.

2. **Tap one of the following options:**

   ● **Select.** Tap to select some of the text. Selection handles appear around the word you tapped.

   ● **Select All.** Tap to select all the text. iPadOS displays the buttons shown in Figure 1.8; if you don't need to modify the selection, skip to Step 4.

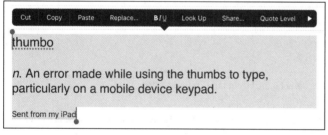

1.8 Select your text and then choose what you want to do with it.

1. **Drag the selection handles to select the text you want to cut or copy.** iPadOS displays a new set of buttons above the text, as well as above the keyboard (see Figure 1.8).

2. **Tap what you want to do with the text:**

   - **Cut.** Removes the text and stores it in memory.

   - **Copy.** Stores a copy of the text in memory.

   1. **If you want to paste the cut or copied text into a different app, open that app.**

   2. **Position the cursor where you want the text to appear.**

   3. **Tap the cursor and then tap Paste (see Figure 1.8).** iPadOS inserts the cut or copied text.

Copying and pasting an image

To make a copy of an image, such as a photo or illustration in a web page, follow these steps:

1. **Long press the image.** iPadOS displays a menu of options.

2. **Tap Copy.** iPadOS copies the image to memory.

3. **Open the app to which you want to paste the copy of the image.**

4. **Position the cursor where you want the image inserted.**

5. **Tap the cursor.**

6. **Tap Paste.** iPadOS pastes the image.

Undoing an edit

The iPad's many editing features give it an almost computer-like feel, but there's another feature that takes it a step closer to computer-hood: Undo. That's right, just like on your regular computer, iPadOS offers an Undo command that can reverse your most recent action, whether it's typing something, deleting some text, or pasting an object you cut or copied. If that typing, deletion, or paste was a mistake, Undo is happy to reverse it for you.

To use Undo, you have two choices:

- Above the keyboard, tap the Undo icon (the left-pointing arrow pointed out earlier in Figure 1.5). Note that the keyboard also offers a Redo icon that undoes the Undo.

- Give your iPad a vigorous shake and you see a dialog similar to the one shown in Figure 1.9. Tap Undo *Action* (where *Action* is whatever type of edit you're reversing, such as Paste or Typing) to reverse your most recent edit.

	Undo Paste	
Cancel		Undo

1.9 Shake your iPad to display the Undo dialog.

Note

If you shake your iPad and nothing happens, it means the Shake to Undo feature is turned off. Open the Settings app, tap Accessibility, tap Touch, and then tap the Shake to Undo switch to On.

Configuring iPad from the Control Center

Your iPad is jammed to the hilt with useful tools and features. That's a good thing, but most of the time those tools require several swipes and a few taps to access. This isn't a big deal for tools you use only every now and then, but it can become tedious if you have one or more tools that you use constantly.

That tedium is likely why the iPadOS programmers decided to fix the problem by creating the Control Center. This is a special screen that offers quick and easy access to no less than 15 of the most useful iPad tools. And when I say "quick and easy," what I really mean is a flick. That is, you flick down from the top right corner of the screen to open the Control Center, as shown in Figure 1.10.

Figure 1.10 points out what each Control Center icon represents, but note that your version of Control Center might display more or fewer icons depending on your iPad model and iPadOS version. I cover most of the Control Center tools elsewhere in the book, so I won't go through each one here. To close the Control Center, tap outside of it.

You can make the Control Center even more useful by customizing the bottom rows. Open the Settings app, tap Control Center, and then add the controls you want to use and remove those you don't.

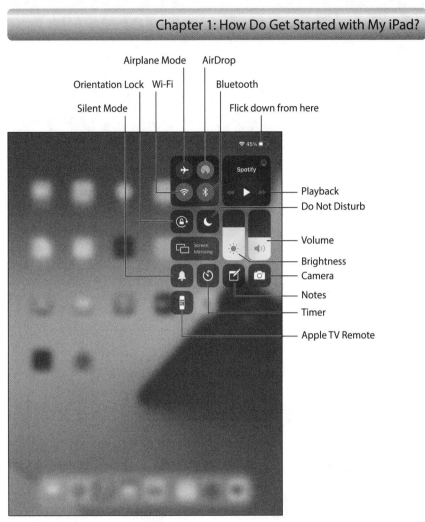

Airplane Mode   AirDrop

Orientation Lock   Wi-Fi   Bluetooth

Silent Mode   Flick down from here

Playback
Do Not Disturb
Volume
Brightness
Camera
Notes
Timer
Apple TV Remote

1.10 The Control Center offers "one-flick" access to some important iPad tools.

How Do I Connect to a Network?

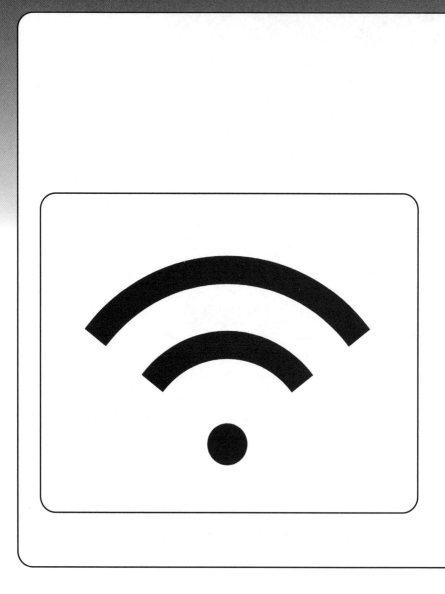

You can do plenty of things on your iPad without having to reach out and touch some remote website or service. You can jot some notes, add appointments, edit contacts, or just play around with the settings. However, I'm willing to bet you didn't fork over the big bucks for your tablet just so you could use the Notes app. Whether you want to go on a web surfin' Safari, visit the App Store or iTunes Store to grab some content, or use Maps to find your way, the iPad comes alive when it's connected to a Wi-Fi or cellular network.

Making Wi-Fi Network Connections

Unless you have an iPad with a cellular antenna (more on that a bit later in this chapter), the only way to get your iPad online is to connect to a nearby Wi-Fi network. Connecting to Wi-Fi is one of the iPad's setup steps, so you might already be good to go. However, if you have multiple Wi-Fi networks or if you take your tablet to a different Wi-Fi location, then you need to know how to connect to another network.

You begin by displaying the list of available Wi-Fi networks using either of the following techniques:

- Open your iPad's Control Center; then long press inside the section that includes the Wi-Fi icon. This expands the section, and you then long press the Wi-Fi icon.

- Open Settings and tap Wi-Fi.

Either way, iPadOS displays a list of available Wi-Fi networks, as shown in Figure 2.1. This list shows you the network name, a lock icon if the network requires a password, and the network's signal strength (the more bars there are, the stronger the signal).

Here are the steps to follow to connect to a Wi-Fi network:

1. **In the list of Wi-Fi networks, tap the network you want to join.** iPadOS prompts you to enter the network's password (if it requires one, as almost all networks do).

2. **Type the password.** Note that iPadOS will remember the password, which enables your iPad to join the same network automatically in the future (unless the password changes).

3. **Tap Join.** iPadOS connects to the network. You now see the Wi-Fi icon in your iPad's status bar, which shows you the network's signal strength.

4. **(Optional)** For a commercial Wi-Fi network — such as one you might access in a hotel or airport — enter your credit card data when prompted (which might not occur until you attempt to access a website or check your email).

2.1 The first step for making a Wi-Fi connection is to see which networks are available.

Displaying nearby Wi-Fi networks automatically

Displaying the list of nearby networks as I describe in the previous section isn't hard, but if you're on the move, you might prefer that iPadOS let you know when a network comes within range. You can configure this by following these steps:

1. **Open the Settings app.**

2. **Tap Wi-Fi.** iPadOS displays the Wi-Fi settings.

3. **Tap Ask to Join Networks.** iPadOS displays the Ask to Join Networks settings.

4. **Tap one of the following:**

   - **Ask.** iPadOS displays a list of nearby networks whenever a new network comes within range of your iPad. You can then select the network you want to join.

   - **Notify.** iPadOS looks for nearby networks that are being accessed by many people. When one of these popular networks comes within range of your tablet, iPadOS lets you know. In the notification that appears, tap Join to connect to the network.

   - **Off.** iPadOS doesn't alert you when nearby networks are available.

Making a connection to a hidden Wi-Fi network

When you display the list of nearby Wi-Fi networks, as I describe earlier in this section, what you see is all the networks that have opted to broadcast their availability. However, a network administrator might choose to not broadcast the network's availability, so even though the network is within range of your iPad, the network's name doesn't appear in the list of nearby networks. Why would a network admin do this? It's a common Wi-Fi security precaution, the rationale being that a network that can't be seen can't be hacked. (Sadly, this measure provides only a marginally more secure network because it's easy for a savvy hacker to still see the network when authorized users connect to it.)

Fortunately, if you know the network's name, its security info, and its password, you can still connect to it manually by following these steps:

1. **Open the Settings app.**

2. **Tap Wi-Fi.** iPadOS displays the Wi-Fi settings.

3. **At the bottom of the list of available networks, tap Other.** iPadOS displays the Other Network dialog, shown in Figure 2.2.

4. **Use the Name box to enter the network's name.**

5. **Tap Security.** iPadOS displays the Security dialog.

6. **Tap the security type the Wi-Fi network uses.** If you're not sure which security type the network uses, select WPA2/WPA3 because that's the most common type.

7. **Tap Back (<).** iPadOS returns you to the Other Network dialog.

8. **Use the Password text box to enter the network password.** Note that if you selected None in Step 6, then you won't see the Password text box.

9. **Tap Join.** iPadOS connects your iPad to the network.

	Enter network information	
Cancel	**Other Network**	Join
Name	Network Name	
Security		WPA2/WPA3 >
Password		

2.2 You can connect to a hidden Wi-Fi network using the Other Network dialog.

Working with Wi-Fi Connections

Wi-Fi is often a set-it-and-forget-it experience because, as I mention earlier, iPadOS remembers the password for a network you join and then connects to that network automatically the next time the network comes within range of your tablet. However, there are a few other Wi-Fi tricks and techniques you should know about, and the next few sections provide the details.

Checking Wi-Fi security

Since Wi-Fi signals can be easily picked up outside your home or office, you need to protect your network with a strong password and a strong security type. For the security type, iPadOS can let you know whether your network is secure. Open Settings, tap Wi-Fi, join your network if you haven't done so already, then tap the network's More Info icon (the circled *i*). If your network is using a weak security type, then you see a Weak Security message like the one shown in Figure 2.3. You (or your network administrator) should configure the network to use the recommended security type. When that's done, tap Forget This Network and then reconnect to your network to take advantage of the enhanced security.

Weak Security

WPA/WPA2 (TKIP) is not considered secure.

If this is your Wi-Fi network, configure the router to use WPA2 (AES) or WPA3 security type.

Learn more about recommended settings for Wi-Fi...

2.3 If your Wi-Fi network isn't using the optimal security type, you see a Weak Security message like the one shown here.

Using Wi-Fi to transfer a file from your Mac to your iPad

If your Mac and iPad are connected to the same Wi-Fi network, you can use AirDrop to transfer a file from your Mac to your tablet. Here are the steps to follow:

1. **On your Mac, open the Finder app and then click AirDrop in the sidebar.** You can also click Go ⇨ AirDrop or press ⌘+Shift+R. An icon for your iPad appears in the AirDrop window.

Note

To check that your iPad has AirDrop turned on, launch Settings, tap General, tap AirDrop and then make sure the Contacts Only option is selected. (If, after a few seconds, you don't see your iPad on your Mac, select Everyone instead.) When the transfer is complete, tap Receiving Off to prevent any unauthorized user from sending you files.

2. **Open another Finder window (choose File ⇨ New Finder Window) and use the new window to locate the file you want to transfer to your iPad.**

3. **Drag the file from the second Finder window; then drop it on the iPad icon in the AirDrop window.** iPadOS either opens the file or asks you to select an app to open the file.

4. **Tap the app you want to use to open the file.** To save the file to the cloud instead of opening it, tap Save to iCloud Drive instead.

Preventing your iPad from automatically joining a known network connection

If you disable a network's Auto-Join feature, as I describe in the previous section, iPadOS still remembers the network's connection data. This means that if you tap the network in the list of available networks, iPadOS will join the network automatically. That's great for a network you might want to join every now and then, but sometimes you *never* want to join a remembered network. Perhaps the network is too slow or has poor security. Whatever the reason, it's best to tell iPadOS to forget the network by following these steps:

1. **Open the Settings app.**

2. **Tap Wi-Fi.** iPadOS displays the Wi-Fi settings.

3. **Tap the More Info icon (the circled *i*) to the right of the network you want to forget.** iPadOS displays the network's settings.

4. **Tap Forget this Network.** iPadOS asks for confirmation.

5. **Tap Forget.** iPadOS discards the connection data for the network.

Shutting off the Wi-Fi antenna

Your iPad uses its built-in Wi-Fi antenna to constantly scan for available Wi-Fi networks, which brings two main advantages:

- You know the list of nearby networks is always up do date.

- It provides greater accuracy to location-based services such as the Maps app.

However, there's also a big disadvantage to this constant network scanning: It drains your iPad's battery. If you won't be joining any Wi-Fi networks for a while, you can reduce the load on your tablet's battery by shutting off the Wi-Fi antenna. Here's how:

1. **Open the Settings app.**

2. **Tap Wi-Fi.** iPadOS displays the Wi-Fi settings.

3. **Tap the Wi-Fi switch to Off.** iPadOS shuts off the Wi-Fi antenna, disconnects from your current network, and no longer scans for nearby networks.

To resume the Wi-Fi thing, repeat these steps to turn the Wi-Fi switch to On.

Genius

An easier way to toggle the Wi-Fi antenna is to display the Control Center and then tap the Wi-Fi icon.

Tethering to an iPhone Internet Connection

If you have a Wi-Fi–only iPad, you might think you're stuck if you're out and about, need to use the Internet, and there's no Wi-Fi in sight. If you have an iPhone with you, then you can work around this problem by using a nifty feature called Personal Hotspot, which enables you to configure your iPhone as a kind of Internet hub or gateway device — something like the hotspots that are available in coffee shops and other public areas.

You can connect your iPad to your iPhone via Wi-Fi, and your tablet can then use the iPhone cellular Internet connection to get online. This is often called *Internet tethering*. The downside is that some providers will charge you extra for tethering. This is slowly changing, but read the fine print on your cellular contract to be sure.

Your first step down the Personal Hotspot road is to activate the feature on your iPhone. Here's how it's done:

1. **Open the Settings app.**

2. **Tap Personal Hotspot.** Your iPhone opens the Personal Hotspot screen.

3. **Tap the Allow Others to Join switch to the On position.**

4. **Tap Wi-Fi Password, enter a password, and then tap Done.**

With Personal Hotspot enabled on your iPhone, follow these steps to connect your iPad to it via Wi-Fi:

1. **Open the Settings app.**

2. **Tap Wi-Fi.** iPadOS displays the Wi-Fi settings. You can also open the Control Center, long press anywhere in the section that includes the Wi-Fi icon, and then long press the Wi-Fi icon.

3. **In the network list, tap the one that has the same name as your iPhone, as shown in Figure 2.4.** Your tablet prompts you for the Wi-Fi password.

4. Type the Personal Hotspot Wi-Fi password and then tap Join. In the status bar, your iPad shows the Personal Hotspot icon, which is two interconnected rings, as shown in Figure 2.5.

2.4 To make a Wi-Fi connection to the iPhone hotspot, display the list of wireless networks and then select the network with the same name as your iPhone.

Personal Hotspot icon

2.5 When your iPad is tethered, it shows the Personal Hotspot icon in the status bar.

Note

If you have a cellular iPad, you can use it as a Personal Hotspot if your data plan allows for Internet tethering. Tap Settings, tap Cellular Data, tap Personal Hotspot, and then tap the Allow Others to Join switch to On.

Working with Cellular-Enabled iPads

Some iPad models come with a cellular chip and antenna that enable those tablets to connect to a cellular network. The big advantage here is that you can use your tablet online even when there's no Wi-Fi within miles of your location. As long as you're within the cellular network's coverage area, you can send and receive email, surf the web, map a location, and perform all your other favorite online activities. The one disadvantage is that cellular connections aren't free. You'll need a data plan from your favorite (if that's the right word) cellular provider.

Tracking cellular data usage

Having a data plan with a cellular provider means never having to worry about getting access to the network. However, unless you're paying for unlimited access (lucky you!), you should be worrying about going over whatever maximum amount of data usage your plan provides per month. That's because going over your data max means you start paying through the nose for each megabyte, and you can run up a hefty bill in no time.

To avoid that, keep track of your cellular data usage by following these steps:

1. **Open the Settings app.**

2. **Tap Cellular.** The Cellular settings appear.

3. **In the Cellular Data section, read the Current Period and Current Period Roaming values.**

4. **If you're at the end of your data period, tap Reset Statistics to get a fresh start for the new period.**

Shutting off the LTE antenna

LTE cellular connections are fast, but they use a lot of battery power because the LTE antenna is constantly scanning for an LTE signal — even if you're on a Wi-Fi network. If your iPad battery is running low, you can switch to the slower — but lower-powered — 3G cellular antenna by following these steps:

1. **Open the Settings app.**

2. **Tap Cellular.** The Cellular settings appear.

3. **Tap Cellular Data Options.**

4. **Tap Voice & Data.** The Voice & Data settings appear.

5. **Tap 3G.** Your iPad shuts off the LTE antenna and turns on the 3G antenna.

Preventing your iPad from using cellular data

If you're bumping up against the monthly ceiling of your iPad's cellular data plan, you'll want to be careful not to exceed your cap because that can get expensive in a hurry. If you don't trust yourself (or anyone who might have access to your iPad), you can just shut off your iPad's access to cellular data. Here are the steps to follow:

1. **Open the Settings app.**

2. **Tap Cellular.** The Cellular settings appear.

3. **Tap the Cellular Data switch to Off.**

Controlling app access to cellular data

Preventing your iPad from using any cellular data, as I describe in the previous section, is a drastic move, particularly if you know that a particular high-bandwidth app (I'm looking at *you*, YouTube!) is causing most of the trouble. In that case, you can configure your iPad to disable access to cellular data app-by-app. Here's how:

1. **Open the Settings app.**

2. **Tap Cellular.** The Cellular settings appear.

3. **In the Cellular Data section, for each app that you want to prevent from using cellular data, tap the app's switch to Off.**

Disabling data roaming

Data roaming lets you surf the web, send and receive email, exchange text messages, and perform all the usual iPad activities while you're outside of your usual cellular coverage area (and not on Wi-Fi, of course). It can be expensive, especially if your iPad runs up huge roaming bills by performing background tasks such as checking email.

To avoid these hidden charges, follow these steps to disable data roaming when you don't need it:

1. **Open the Settings app.**

2. **Tap Cellular.** The Cellular settings appear.

3. **Tap Cellular Data Options.**

4. **Tap the Data Roaming switch to Off.**

Switching to Low Data Mode

If your cellular data usage is inching perilously close to your plan's maximum, switch to Low Data Mode, which tells iPadOS to stop performing tasks such as automatic updates and photo syncing. Here are the steps to follow to switch to Low Data Mode:

1. **Open the Settings app.**

2. **Tap Cellular.** The Cellular settings appear.

3. **Tap Cellular Data Options.**

4. **Tap the Low Data Mode switch to On.**

Activating Airplane Mode

When you're flying in a commercial airplane, wireless signals are almost always disallowed. That's fine with you because your iPad has tons of features and apps that don't require a wireless connection. However, your iPad still broadcasts wireless signals even when you're not using Wi-Fi, Bluetooth, or the cellular network. You could turn off these signals manually, but an easier way is to put your iPad into Airplane Mode, which disables your iPad's components that receive and transmit wireless data.

Caution

If you activate Airplane Mode and then enable Wi-Fi or Bluetooth (or both), iPadOS remembers this and enables those components the next time you activate Airplane Mode. That's a nice feature, but beware: Having either of these antennas enabled might be frowned upon by your current airline. To avoid trouble, make sure none of the iPad's antennas is still enabled when you activate Airplane Mode.

To activate Airplane Mode, use either of the following techniques:

- **Open the Settings app and then tap the Airplane Mode switch to On.**

- **Open the Control Center and then tap to activate the Airplane Mode icon.**

When Airplane Mode is activated, you see the Airplane Mode icon in the status bar (where the Signal Strength and Network icons would normally appear), as shown in Figure 2.6.

Airplane Mode icon

2.6 The Airplane Mode icon appears in the status bar when Airplane Mode is activated.

Connecting Bluetooth Devices

Bluetooth is a wireless technology that enables your iPad to make wireless connections to other Bluetooth-enabled devices. When you bring the Bluetooth device to within 33 feet of your iPad (that's the maximum Bluetooth range), they connect when the following criteria are met:

- **Both devices are discoverable.** Bluetooth devices only broadcast their availability to connect — that is, the devices make themselves *discoverable* — when you say so. So, nothing can happen until you make both your iPad and the Bluetooth device discoverable.

- **You pair the iPad and the device.** Just because both your iPad and your Bluetooth device are discoverable, it doesn't follow that the connection is automatic. The connection happens only when you *pair* your iPad with the other device. In some cases, this pairing requires you to enter a multidigit *passkey* into the Bluetooth device (as long as the device has a keypad of some kind). Otherwise, you pair the devices by tapping a Pair button that your iPad displays.

Making your iPad discoverable

You make your iPad discoverable by turning on its Bluetooth transceiver. That radio is on by default, but it doesn't hurt to follow these steps to make sure:

1. **Open the Settings app.**

2. **Tap Bluetooth.** The Bluetooth settings appear.

3. **Tap the Bluetooth switch to On, as shown in Figure 2.7.**

Bluetooth

Bluetooth

Now discoverable as "iPad".

MY DEVICES

2.7 Tapping the Bluetooth switch to On makes your iPad discoverable.

Pairing with a Bluetooth keyboard

If you want to use a physical keyboard with your tablet, iPadOS supports connections to Bluetooth keyboards. When you pair your iPad and a Bluetooth keyboard, the on-screen keyboard is disabled. Here are the steps to follow to pair your iPad and a Bluetooth keyboard:

1. **Open the Settings app.**

2. **Tap Bluetooth.** The Bluetooth screen appears.

3. **Press the button or turn on the switch that makes your Bluetooth keyboard discoverable.** After anywhere from a few seconds to a minute or so, the keyboard appears in the Bluetooth screen.

4. **Tap the Bluetooth keyboard.** iPadOS displays a passkey like the one shown in Figure 2.8.

Bluetooth Pairing Request

Enter this code on "Microsoft Bluetooth Mobile Keyboard 6000", followed by the return or enter key.

7343

Cancel

2.8 Your iPad displays a passkey for pairing with the Bluetooth keyboard.

5. **Using the Bluetooth keyboard, type the passkey and then press Return (or Enter).** iPadOS pairs with the keyboard. In the Bluetooth screen, you now see *Connected* beside the keyboard.

Pairing with Bluetooth headphones

Bluetooth headphones (or headsets, which also include a microphone for talking) are great because there are no wires to get in the way of listening to music or podcasts or whatever. Here are the steps to follow to pair your iPad with Bluetooth headphones:

1. **Open the Settings app.**

2. **Tap Bluetooth.** The Bluetooth screen appears.

3. **Press the button or turn on the switch that makes your Bluetooth headphones discoverable.** Wait until you see the name of your headphones show up in the Bluetooth screen.

4. **Tap the Bluetooth headphones.** Most of the time, iPadOS pairs with the headphones automatically. If you see *Connected* beside the device in the Bluetooth screen, skip the rest of these steps; otherwise, you see the Enter PIN dialog.

5. **Type the headphone's passkey.** See the documentation that came with your headphones to get the passkey (it's usually 0000).

6. **Tap Done.** Your iPad pairs with the headphones.

Selecting paired headphones as the audio output device

When you pair Bluetooth headphones with your iPad, iPadOS sets the headphones as the default audio output device. In some rare instances that change doesn't happen, but you can follow these steps to set the Bluetooth headphones as your iPad's default audio output device:

1. **Open the Control Center.**

2. **Tap the AirPlay icon.** This icon appears in the top right corner of the playback controls. The AirPlay dialog appears.

3. **Tap your paired Bluetooth headphones.** You see a check mark beside the headphones, as shown in Figure 2.9, and your iPad starts playing audio through the headphones.

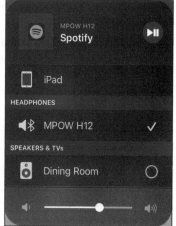

2.9 Use the AirPlay screen to select your paired Bluetooth headphones.

Unpairing your iPad from a Bluetooth device

If you don't want to use a Bluetooth device any longer or if you want to pair the device with another device, you should unpair it from your iPad. Follow these steps:

1. **Open the Settings app.**

2. **Tap Bluetooth.** The Bluetooth screen appears.

3. **Tap the More Info icon (the circled *i*) to the right of the Bluetooth device name.**

4. **Tap Forget this Device.** iPadOS unpairs the device.

How Do I Configure My iPad?

If you've made your way through the first two chapters of this book, then you know your way around your iPad, and you're connected to a network. What else could anyone need? You'd be surprised. Although the iPad works like a champ right out of the box, even champs can improve their game. You may find that the default settings make sense for the average user, but you're far from average — after all, you bought this book! This chapter shows you how to configure your tablet to work the way you do.

Customizing the iPad Home Screen

The iPad's Home screen is simple to use (just tap an app icon to run that app), but chances are it's not configured completely to your liking. Not to worry: The next few sections take you through a few useful techniques for making the Home screen your own.

Rearranging the Home screen icons

How can you make the Home screen more efficient? There are two main ways:

- **Move your most-used icons to the Dock.** This is the horizontal section that appears at the bottom of each Home screen. Depending on your iPad, you can add between 11 and 15 icons here.

- **Move your other often-used icons to a single screen for quick access.** Depending on your settings, you can add up to either 20 or 30 icons to a single Home screen.

Genius

With iPadOS, you can choose Home screen icons that are either bigger (up to 20 per screen) or smaller (up to 30 per screen). To set this, open the Settings app, tap Home Screen & Dock, and then tap either More (to use smaller icons) or Bigger.

To rearrange your iPad's Home screen icons for greater efficiency, follow these steps:

1. **Display any Home screen.**

2. **Long press any Home screen icon.** iPadOS displays a list of commands you can run.

3. **Tap Edit Home Screen.** The Home screen icons start wiggling.

4. **Drag the icons into whatever positions you prefer.** Here are some notes to bear in mind if you want to move an icon to another screen:

   - To move an app icon to a previous screen, first drag the icon to the left edge of the current screen.

   - To move an app icon to a later screen, first drag the icon to the right edge of the current screen.

   - Either way, once the new screen appears, drag the icon to the position you want.

5. **Reorder the Dock icons by dragging them to the left or to the right.** Note that you can't drag an icon to the right of the Dock separator.

6. **To add a Dock icon, drag any Home screen icon into the Dock.** Make sure you add the icon to the left of the Dock separator.

7. **To remove an icon from the Dock, drag the icon off the Dock.**

8. **To remove an icon from the Recent Apps section, tap the minus sign (–) that appears in the top right corner of the icon.**

Genius

If you find you rarely use the Recent Apps section of the Dock, you should turn it off to gain some extra real estate for your other Dock icons. Open the Settings app, tap Home Screen & Dock, and then tap the Show Suggested and Recent Apps in Dock switch to Off.

9. **Stop the Home screen editing by tapping Done or by tapping an empty part of any Home screen.** iPadOS saves the new icon arrangement.

Storing multiple app icons in an app folder

An *app folder* is a special Home screen icon that can store multiple app icons. This is an easy way to organize your Home screen so that related apps are grouped under a single icon. This not only makes your apps easier to find, but also reduces Home screen clutter. To create and populate an app folder, follow these steps:

1. **Display the screen that contains at least one of the apps you want in your folder.**

2. **Long press any Home screen icon.** iPadOS displays a list of actions you can perform.

3. **Tap Edit Home Screen.** The icons start wiggling.

4. **Drag an icon that you want in the folder and drop it on another icon that you want in the same folder.** iPadOS creates the folder.

5. **Tap the folder.** iPadOS displays a text box that displays the default folder name, as shown in Figure 3.1.

6. **Edit the folder name and then tap Done.**

7. **Stop the Home screen editing by tapping Done or by tapping an empty part of any Home screen.** iPadOS saves the new icon arrangement.

3.1 To create an app folder, drop one app icon on another.

To launch an app from the new folder, tap the folder to open it and then tap the app. To work with your app folders, long press any icon, tap Edit Home Screen, and then use the following techniques:

- **Add another app.** Drag the app icon and drop it on the folder.

- **Rename the folder.** Tap the folder to open it and then edit the folder name.

- **Rearrange the folder icons.** Tap the folder to open it; then drag and drop the app icons to the new positions within the folder.

- **Remove an app.** Tap the folder to open it; then drag the icon out of the folder.

Adding a web page icon to the Home screen

If you have a web page that you visit frequently, a fast way to access that page is to add an icon for the page to your iPad's Home screen. To save a web page as a Home screen icon, follow these steps:

1. **Use Safari to display the page you want to save.**

2. **Tap Share (the icon with the arrow).** iPadOS displays a list of actions.

3. **Tap Add to Home Screen.** iPadOS prompts you to edit the icon name.

4. **Edit the name as needed.**

5. **Tap Add.** iPadOS adds the icon to the Home screen.

Genius

If you overdo it with the Home screen customizations, you might want to get a fresh start by resetting the Home screen icons back to the default layout. See Chapter 12 to learn how to do this.

Dealing with App Notifications

Many apps change regularly with new content, updated settings, new features, and more. How do you know about these changes? Most of the time, you don't, unless you run the app and notice that something is new. A much better way to learn what's new with an app is to get *notifications* from the app, which are messages that the app displays on your iPad. These messages come in the following four varieties:

- **Sounds.** These are sound effects that play when some app-related event occurs.

- **Alerts.** These are messages that pop up on your screen and stay there until you tap a button to dismiss them.

- **Banners.** These are messages that appear at the top of the screen and then disappear after a few seconds.

- **Badges.** These are red circles that appear in the upper right corner of app icons. The badge usually displays a number in white text, the interpretation of which depends on the app. For example, the Mail app badge tells you the number of unread messages you have waiting for you.

Apps can't display notifications on your iPad unless you give them permission. To do that, the first time you start an app that supports notifications, you see a message similar to the one shown in Figure 3.2. If you want to see notifications from the app, tap Allow; otherwise, tap Don't Allow.

Opening the Notification Center

iPadOS not only displays notifications as they happen, but also stores all your recent alerts and banners in the Notification Center. So, if you miss a banner or are wondering what else might be going on with your app notifications, you can display the Notification Center and get caught up.

To display the Notification Center, swipe down from the top edge of the iPad screen. The screen that appears displays your recent notifications grouped by app. From here, you can either work with your notifications (as I describe in the next section) or close the Notification Center by swiping up from the bottom of the screen.

"Flickr" Would Like to Send You Notifications

Notifications may include alerts, sounds, and icon badges. These can be configured in Settings.

Don't Allow   Allow

3.2 iPadOS asks for your permission to allow notifications from an app.

Working with notifications

With the Notification Center on-screen, here are the techniques you can use to work with your notifications:

- **Open the item.** Tap the notification to launch the associated app and open the item the notification deals with.

- **View a notification.** Long press the notification (or swipe left on the notification) and then tap the View command that appears. When you view a notification, you usually get a few more buttons that offer other tasks for handling the notification. For example, if you view a notification from the Mail app for an email message, you see two buttons: Trash and Mark as Read (see Figure 3.3).

3.3 Viewing a notification usually displays one or more buttons, such as the Trash and Mark as Read buttons for this email notification.

Manage the app's notifications. Swipe left on a notification and then tap Manage, which offers three more actions:

- **Deliver Quietly.** Tells the app to no longer play a sound or display a banner or badge when it receives new notifications.

- **Turn Off.** Tells the app to cease delivering notifications.

- **Settings.** Opens the Settings app and displays the app's notification settings (described in the next section).

Clear a notification. Swipe left on the notification and then tap Clear.

Clear all grouped notifications. If the app's notifications are grouped in Notification Center, swipe left on the group and then tap Clear All.

Configuring an app's notifications

iPadOS offers quite a few settings for customizing an app's notifications. For example, you can enable or disable most notification types (sounds, alerts, and badges), set the banner style, and even disable an app's notifications altogether.

Here's how to customize an app's notifications:

1. **Open the Settings app.**

2. **Tap Notifications.** The Notifications settings appear.

3. **Tap the app you want to configure.** The app's notification settings appear. Figure 3.4 shows the settings for the Reminders app. You should note, however, that not all apps support every possible setting.

4. **To not receive any notifications from the app, tap the Allow Notifications switch to Off.** Settings hides all the notification settings for the app, so you can skip the rest of these steps.

5. **In the Alerts section, activate the check box for each place where you want to see alerts from the app.** Your choices are Lock Screen, Notification Center, and Banners.

6. **If you activated the Banners check box in Step 5, tap Banner Style and then tap the banner type you prefer:**

- **Temporary.** Each banner disappears automatically after a few seconds.

- **Persistent.** Each banner stays on-screen until you dismiss it.

Settings

Q Search

PM Paul McFedries
Apple ID, iCloud, Media &...

AppleCare+ Coverage Availa... >

There are 50 days remaining to add
AppleCare+ coverage for this iPad.

✈ Airplane Mode

📶 Wi-Fi   Logophilia5

✶ Bluetooth   On

🔔 Notifications

🔈 Sounds

🌙 Do Not Disturb

< Notifications   **Reminders**

Allow Notifications

ALERTS

9:41

Lock Screen   Notification Center   Banners
    ✓   ✓   ✓

Banner Style   Persistent >

Sounds   Chord >

Badges

OPTIONS

Show Previews   Always (Default) >

Notification Grouping   Automatic >

3.4 iPadOS offers per-app customization of the notification settings.

7. **For an app that offers sound notifications, configure this notification type by using one of the following:**

   • **Sounds menu.** Tap this menu to choose a sound to play. Alternatively, tap None in the menu to play no sound.

   • **Sounds switch.** Tap this switch to toggle sound notifications for the app on or off.

8. **For an app that supports badges, use the Badges switch to toggle Badges notifications On or Off.**

9. **To configure when you want the app's notifications to show a preview of the item associated with the notification (such as an email message), tap Show Previews and then tap one of the following:**

   • **Always.** You can see a notification preview when your iPad is both locked and unlocked.

- **When Unlocked.** You can only see a notification preview when your iPad isn't locked.

- **Never.** Disables the preview feature.

10. **For an app that supports the grouping of notifications, tap Notification Grouping to select how the app's notifications are grouped in the Notification Center.**

Configuring Do Not Disturb settings

If you and your iPad are in a location where the sounds of an incoming notification would disturb people nearby, you might consider activating Airplane Mode, which turns off all the tablet's antennas. This ensures that you're distraction-free for a while. However, without any working antennas, your iPad can't communicate with the world, so it doesn't download messages or perform any other online activities. That might be what you want, but it's less than optimum if you're expecting something important.

A better way to go is to activate Do Not Disturb mode, which prevents your iPad from making any notification sounds (as well as sounds from other apps, such as text messages). However, your iPad remains online and continues to receive incoming data, so when you're ready to get back to work, you can get up to speed quickly.

To turn on Do Not Disturb, you have two choices:

- Open the Settings app, tap Do Not Disturb, and then tap the Do Not Disturb switch to On.

- Open the Control Center and tap Do Not Disturb (pointed out in Figure 1.10).

However, you can also customize Do Not Disturb by following these steps:

1. **Open the Settings app.**

2. **Tap Do Not Disturb.** The Do Not Disturb settings appear.

3. **To schedule a time when iPadOS automatically starts and stops Do Not Disturb, tap the Scheduled switch to On.** You then use the following controls to set up the schedule:

   - **From.** Sets the time you want iPadOS to start Do Not Disturb.

   - **To.** Sets the time you want iPadOS to end Do Not Disturb.

   - **Dim Lock screen.** Tap this switch to On to have iPadOS indicate that Do Not Disturb is activated by darkening the Lock screen. (Although note that iPadOS always displays a Lock screen message telling you when Do Not Disturb mode is activated.)

4. **To configure Do Not Disturb to silence notifications only when your iPad is locked, tap the While iPad is Locked option.**

5. **To configure Do Not Disturb to allow certain calls, tap Allow Calls From and then tap who can get through to you even when Do Not Disturb is activated: Everyone, No One, or a particular contact group.**

6. **To configure Do Not Disturb to allow a call when someone calls twice within three minutes (meaning it might be an emergency), leave Repeated Calls in the On position.**

Trying Out a Few More Useful iPad Customizations

The rest of this chapter takes you through a few more practical and useful iPad customization techniques.

Changing your iPad's name

The name of your iPad doesn't come up all that often, but it does appear in your iCloud backups, in lists of nearby Bluetooth devices, and similar situations. So, it's probably a good idea to ensure your iPad has a unique name. Here's how:

1. **Open the Settings app.**

2. **Tap General.** The General settings appear.

3. **Tap About.** The About page appears.

4. **Tap Name.** Settings displays the current name of your iPad in a text box.

5. **Edit the name as needed.**

Customizing iPad sounds

Your iPad makes a lot of noises sometimes, most of which are useful. However, if you think your iPad is a little too chatty, you can customize which sounds your iPad utters by following these steps:

1. **Open the Settings app.**

2. **Tap Sounds.** The Sounds settings appear.

3. **If you use headphones with your iPad, tap Reduce Loud Sounds, tap the Reduce Loud Sounds switch to On, and then select a decibel value.** iPadOS will monitor the headphones' audio and automatically turn down any sounds that are over the decibel value you selected.

4. **Drag the Ringer and Alerts slider to set the volume of the ringtone that plays when a call comes in.**

5. **To lock the ringer volume, tap the Change with Buttons switch to Off.** This means that pressing the volume buttons on the side of the iPad will have no effect on the ringer volume.

6. **For each of the events in the Sounds list, tap the event and then tap the sound you want to hear.** To turn off the event sound, instead, tap None.

7. **To silence the (truly annoying) sound your iPad makes when you tap a key on the virtual keyboard, tap the Keyboard Clicks switch to Off.**

8. **To silence the sound your iPad makes when you lock and unlock it, tap the Lock Sound switch to Off.**

Customizing the iPad keyboard

Did you know that the keyboard changes depending on the app you use? For example, the regular keyboard features a spacebar at the bottom. However, if you're entering an email address in the Mail app, the keyboard that appears offers a smaller spacebar and uses the extra space to show an at sign (@) key and a period (.) key, two characters that are part of any email address. Nice! Here are some other nice innovations you get with the iPad keyboard:

- **Auto-Capitalization.** If you type a punctuation mark that indicates the end of a sentence — for example, a period (.), a question mark (?), or an exclamation mark (!) — or if you press Return to start a new paragraph, the iPad automatically activates the Shift key, because it assumes you're starting a new sentence.

- **Double-tapping the spacebar.** This activates a keyboard shortcut: Instead of entering two spaces, the iPad automatically enters a period (.) followed by a space. This is a welcome bit of efficiency because otherwise you'd have to tap the Number key (123) to display the numbers and punctuation marks, tap the period (.), and then tap the spacebar.

Genius

Typing a number or punctuation mark normally requires three taps: tapping Number (123), tapping the number or symbol, and then tapping ABC. Here's a faster way: Use one finger to tap and hold the Number key to open the numeric keyboard, use a second finger to tap the number or punctuation symbol you want, and then release the Number key. This types the number or symbol and returns you to the regular keyboard.

● **Auto-Correction.** For many people, one of the keys to quick iPad typing is to clear the mind and just tap away without worrying about accuracy. In many cases, you'll actually be rather amazed at how accurate this willy-nilly approach can be. Why does it work? The secret is the Auto-Correction feature on your iPad, which eyeballs what you're typing and automatically corrects any errors. For example, if you type *hte,* your iPad automatically corrects this to *the.* Your iPad displays the suggested correction before you complete the word (say, by tapping a space or a comma), and you can reject the suggestion by tapping the typed text that appears with quotation marks in the predictive typing bar. If you find you never use the predictive suggestions, you can turn them off to save a bit of screen real estate.

● **Caps Lock.** One thing the iPad keyboard doesn't seem to have is a Caps Lock feature that, when activated, enables you to type all-uppercase letters. To do this, you need to tap and hold the Shift key and then use a different finger to tap the uppercase letters. However, the iPad actually does have a Caps Lock feature: Double-tap Shift to turn Caps Lock on (which is indicated on the Shift key with a horizontal bar under the arrow) and then tap Shift to turn Caps Lock off.

● **Slide to Type.** If you're *really* in a hurry, you might resent the split second that elapses between the tap of each key. To shave even that small amount of time off your typing chores, you can use the *slide to type* feature, where instead of tapping each key individually, you quickly slide your finger from one letter to the next, only lifting your finger when you complete each word. (Yep, iPadOS adds a space automatically.) It takes a bit of getting used to, but it can make entering text crazy-fast.

Note

Slide to Type only works with the iPad's floating keyboard layout, which I discuss a bit later in this section.

● **Character preview.** This feature displays a pop-up version of each character as you tap it. This is great for iPad keyboard rookies because it helps them be sure they're typing accurately, but veterans often find it distracting. Some even complain that it's a security risk because the letters pop up even when you're typing a password! That might be why Apple chooses to turn off character preview by default, but you can turn it back on if you miss it.

To change the settings for any of these keyboard features, follow these steps:

1. **Open the Settings app.**

2. **Tap General.** The General screen appears.

3. **Tap Keyboard.** The Keyboard screen appears.

4. **Use the switches — including Auto-Capitalization, Auto-Correction, Enable Caps Lock, Predictive, Slide to Type, Character Preview, and "." Shortcut — to toggle keyboard features off and on as you prefer.**

Typing while holding your tablet gets a whole lot easier if you split the on-screen keyboard into two halves — one that appears on the left side of the screen and one that appears on the right. Because both halves are within reaching distance of all but the shortest thumbs, you can type on and hold your tablet simultaneously.

Another on-screen keyboard conundrum is that, in many apps, the keyboard always appears docked at the bottom of the screen, but the text you are typing appears at (or near) the top of the screen. This relatively huge distance between keyboard and text makes it more difficult to type accurately and quickly. Once again, however, iPadOS rides to the rescue, enabling you to undock the keyboard and position this so-called *floating* keyboard anywhere on the screen.

Splitting and floating are controlled by a single setting, so you might want to first follow these steps to ensure this setting is turned on:

1. **Open the Settings app.**

2. **Tap General.** The General screen appears.

3. **Tap Keyboard.** The Keyboard screen appears.

4. **Tap the Split Keyboard switch to On.**

The next time the on-screen keyboard comes up, tap and hold the Hide Keyboard button, which appears in the lower right corner of the keyboard. After a couple of seconds, you see the options shown in Figure 3.5.

Leave your finger on the screen and slide it up to one of the following:

Hide Keyboard

- **Undock.** Tap this option to undock the keyboard and display it in the middle of the screen. To move the keyboard to the position you prefer, drag the Hide Keyboard button. To return to the normal keyboard layout, tap and hold the Hide Keyboard button and then slide your finger up to Dock.

3.5 Tap and hold the Hide Keyboard button to see these options.

- **Split.** Tap this option to undock the keyboard and split it in two halves, as shown in Figure 3.6. Again, you can move the split keyboard to a new position by dragging the Hide Keyboard button. To return to the normal keyboard layout, tap and hold the Hide Keyboard button and then slide your finger up to Dock & Merge.

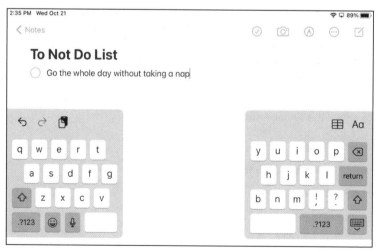

3.6 Tap Split to split the keyboard for easier thumb typing.

● **Floating.** Tap this option to undock the keyboard and display a simpler, smaller version that floats on the screen, as shown in Figure 3.7. To move the floating keyboard around the screen, drag the bar at the bottom of the keyboard. To return to the regular keyboard, drag the floating keyboard to the bottom of the screen.

Configuring the Siri voice assistant

You can make things happen on your iPad via voice commands by using the Siri app, which not only lets you launch apps, but also gives you voice control over web searching, appointments, contacts, reminders, map navigation, text messages, notes, and much more.

First, make sure that Siri is activated by tapping Settings in the Home screen, tapping Siri & Search, and then doing one of the following:

Drag here to move the floating keyboard

3.7 Tap Floating to float the keyboard so that you can easily move it out of the way of your text.

● If your iPad doesn't have a Home button, tap the Press Top Button for Siri switch to On.

● For all other iPad models, tap the Press Home for Siri switch to On.

Either way, when iPadOS asks you to confirm that you want to use Siri, tap Enable Siri.

While you're here, you might want to tap the Listen for "Hey Siri" switch to On (and then run through a brief setup procedure), which makes it even easier to start Siri. Also, you should tell Siri who you are so that when you use references such as "home" and "work," Siri knows what you're talking about. In the Siri & Search screen, tap My Information, and then tap your item in the Contacts list.

You crank up Siri by using any of the following techniques:

● Saying "Hey Siri" (assuming you enabled this feature in the Siri settings).

● Pressing and holding either the Top button (if your iPad doesn't have a Home button) or the Home button.

- Pressing and holding the Mic button on your iPad headphones.
- Pressing and holding the Mic equivalent on a Bluetooth headset.

Siri is often easier to use if you define relationships within it. So, for example, instead of saying "Call Sandy Evans," you can simply say "Call mom." You can define relationships in two ways:

- **Within the Contacts app.** Open the Contacts app, tap your contact item, tap Edit, tap Add Related Name, and then tap the relationship you want to use. Tap the blue More icon to open the All Contacts list and then tap the person you want to add to the field.

- **Within Siri.** Say "*Name* is my *relationship*," where *Name* is the person's name as given in your Contacts list, and *relationship* is the connection, such as *wife, husband, spouse, partner, brother, sister, mother,* or *father.* When Siri asks you to confirm, say "Yes."

Configuring and using multitasking

True multitasking means seeing and working with two or more apps at the same time. Your iPad supports multitasking apps in two ways:

- **Slide Over.** This feature enables you to open an app so that it appears over whatever app you already have on-screen. To use Slide Over, follow these steps:

  1. **Swipe up from the bottom of the screen.** The Dock appears.
  2. **Tap and hold the Dock icon for the app you want to open.**
  3. **Drag the icon up into the screen.** iPadOS opens the app and displays it on top of the current app. To move the app, drag the bar that appears at the top of the app window.

Genius

If you have an app open in Slide Over, you can temporarily move it off-screen by dragging the app's top bar off the right edge of the screen. To bring the app back, swipe left from the right edge of the screen.

- **Split View.** This feature enables you to open two apps side-by-side. To use Split View, follow these steps:

  1. **Open the first app.**

  2. **Swipe up from the bottom of the screen.** The Dock appears.

  3. **Tap and hold the Dock icon for the app you want to open.**

  4. **Drag the icon up and then to either the left or right edge of the screen.** iPadOS opens the app and splits the screen vertically to show both apps at the same time.

These multitasking features are enabled by default, but you can follow these steps to make sure:

1. **On the Home screen, tap Settings to open the Settings app.**

2. **Tap Home Screen & Dock.** The Home screen settings appear.

3. **Tap Multitasking.** The Multitasking settings appear.

4. **Tap the Allow Multiple Apps switch to On.**

I introduce touchscreen gestures in Chapter 1, but I don't cover all of them. The following extra multitasking-related gestures are actually quite useful:

- **When you're running an app, pinch four or five fingers to return to the Home screen.** This feels more natural than pressing an off-screen button to get back to the Home screen.

- **Swipe left or right with four or five fingers to switch between running apps.** This is often a better technique than using the multitasking bar to switch apps because you can see each app as you swipe.

These gestures are turned on by default, but you can follow these steps to make sure that's the case:

1. **On the Home screen, tap Settings to open the Settings app.**

2. **Tap Home Screen & Dock.** The Home screen settings appear.

3. **Tap Multitasking.** The Multitasking settings appear.

4. **Tap the Gestures switch to On.**

Controlling your iPad's privacy settings

Third-party apps occasionally request permission to use the data from another app. For example, an app might need access to your contacts, your calendars, your photos, or your Twitter and Facebook accounts. You can always deny these requests, of course, but if you've allowed access to an app in the past, you might later change your mind and decide you'd prefer to revoke that access. Fortunately, iPadOS offers a Privacy feature that enables you to control which apps have access to your data. Here's how it works:

1. **Open the Settings app.**

2. **Tap Privacy.** The Privacy screen appears.

3. **Tap the app or feature for which you want to control access.** Your iPad displays a list of third-party apps that have requested access to the app or feature.

4. **To revoke a third-party app's access to the app or feature, tap its switch to Off.**

Configuring your iPad to use Apple Pay

If you'd like to use your iPad to pay for stuff without having to press any buttons or insert a payment card, then you need to configure Apply Pay on your tablet. Here's what you do:

1. **Open the Settings app.**

2. **Tap Wallet & Apple Pay.** The Wallet & Apple Pay screen appears.

3. **Tap Add Card.**

4. **Tap Continue.** iPadOS displays a camera frame.

5. **Place your payment card on a flat surface and then position the camera frame so that the card fills the frame.** You might have to hover the frame over the card for a few seconds before iPadOS recognizes it and displays the Card Details screen.

6. **Double-check that your name and card number are accurate; then tap Next.** If either or both of your name and card number contain an error, edit as needed and then tap Next.

7. **Select the card's expiration month and year (if needed; these should already be entered for you), type the card's three-digit security code, and then tap Next.** iPadOS displays some terms and conditions.

8. **Read the terms and conditions (I jest, of course) and then tap Agree.**

9. **If your card requires verification, tap the method you prefer to use (such as Text Message), tap Next, and then enter the verification code when you receive it.** Note that if your verification device is the same iPad as the one you're using, iPadOS will enter the verification code for you automatically.

10. **The next steps depend on whether you're adding your first card or a subsequent card:**

    ● **You're adding your first payment card.** iPadOS adds the payment card to your iPhone's digital wallet and then shows a screen with instructions on using Apple Pay. Tap Continue. iPadOS returns you to the Wallet & Apple Pay screen.

    ● **You're adding a subsequent payment card.** iPadOS asks if you want this new card to be the default for payments. If so, tap Use as Default Card; otherwise, tap Not Now. iPadOS adds the payment card to your iPhone's digital wallet and then returns you to the Wallet & Apple Pay screen.

11. **If you want to add more payment cards, repeat Steps 3 through 10.**

You might be wondering how you pay for something when you have multiple payment cards. Here's how:

● To pay with the default card, double-press either the Top button (if your iPad has Face ID) or the Home button, verify that it's you (with Face ID, Touch ID, or a passcode), and then hold the tablet near the contactless reader until the transaction is complete.

● To pay with another card, double-press either the Top button (if your iPad has Face ID) or the Home button and then verify that it's you (with Face ID, Touch ID, or a passcode). You now see a screen that shows your default card at the top and your other cards at the bottom. Tap the bottom cards, tap the card you want to use, and then hold the phone near the contactless reader until the transaction is complete.

Note Face ID obviously won't work if you're wearing a mask! In that case, iPadOS enables you to use a secondary verification method, such as your passcode.

Genius To specify a different payment card as the default, follow Steps 1 and 2 to open the Wallet & Apple Pay screen, tap Default Card, and then tap the card you prefer to use as the default.

How Can I Get More Out of Web Surfing?

When Apple first announced the iPad, one of the presenters was demonstrating the iPad's Safari web browser and summarized the experience with a terrific line: "It just feels right to hold the Internet in your hands." That's about as succinct a description of web surfing on the iPad as you're ever going to come across, not just because it's perfect in its pithiness, but also because the iPad just might be the ultimate web surfing tool. It's portable, fast, and intuitive, and it offers *no* compromises — it shows actual, full-size web pages, rendered as each site designer intended. However, that doesn't mean you can't make browsing on your iPad even better. This chapter takes you through my favorite tools and techniques for getting even more out of web surfing on your iPad.

Surfing with the Touchscreen

The case in favor of crowning the iPad the best web surfing appliance ever isn't hard to make: It's blazingly fast, it renders most sites perfectly, and the large screen means you almost always see a complete (horizontally, at least) view of the regular version of each page, rather than a partial view or an ugly, dumbed-down mobile version.

The touchscreen is the key to efficient and fun web surfing on your tablet, so here are a few touchscreen tips that can make web surfing even easier and more pleasurable:

- **Double-tap to zoom in and out.** If a web page has identifiable sections (such as paragraphs, images, or tables), you can double-tap a section to have Safari zoom in on that section to fill the width of the screen. Double-tap the screen to zoom back out to the regular magnification.

- **Tap to scroll quickly to the top.** If you find yourself near the bottom of a long web page, it might take you quite a few swipes to return to the top of the page. A faster and easier method is to tap the Safari status bar at the top of the screen, which tells Safari to automatically scroll back to the top of the page.

- **Long press to see a link's location and preview.** Before you tap a link in a web page, you might want to know the link's location (that is, the address of the page referenced by the link). You can see where a link will take you and also eyeball a page preview by long pressing the link. Safari opens a dialog that shows you the domain of the link and offers a thumbnail preview of the linked page. Figure 4.1 shows an example. If the link looks like something you want to check out, tap Open. Alternatively, tap Open in New Window to open the page in a second window that appears beside the current window. If you decide against checking out the link, tap another part of the screen to close the dialog.

- **Long press to copy a link's address.** Copying a link's address to memory is a good idea if you want to include the address in a note, a text, or an email. Long press the link to display the dialog shown in Figure 4.1; then tap Copy. Switch to the other app, tap the app's cursor, and then tap the Paste command that appears.

- **Easy access to some top-level domains.** In Internet-speak, a *top-level domain* (TLD) is the chunk of a domain name that comes after (and includes) the last dot. For example, in apple.com, the *.com* is the TLD. When you're typing in Safari's address bar and you get to the point where you want to enter the TLD, long press the period (.) key. A pop-up appears with keys for the TLDs .edu, .com, .net, and .org, and another for your current country TLD (such as .us for the United States). Slide your finger up and over to the TLD you want to insert.

Domain of the linked page

4.1 Long press a link to see its domain, a thumbnail preview, and some useful link-related commands.

Utilizing Pro Tips for Easier Web Browsing

Browsing the web is everybody's favorite way of wasting time, er, I mean locating useful information. I don't know anyone who doesn't spend huge chunks of time every day surfing the web. And the iPad makes it even easier to browse the day away by enabling you to surf whenever an accessible Wi-Fi network is within range. The more time you spend with Safari on your iPad, the greater the need for your surfing sessions to be easier, faster, and more efficient. The touchscreen tips from the previous section are a good start, but in this section you learn quite a few more tips and techniques for speeding up your surfing.

Browsing with tabs

These days, it's a rare web surfer who marches sequentially through a series of web pages. In your own surfing sessions, you probably leave a few web pages open full time (for things like Google searches and social media feed monitoring). It's also likely that you'll come across a lot of links that you want to check out while leaving the original page open in the browser. In your computer's web browser, you probably handle these and similar surfing situations by launching a tab for each page you want to leave open in the browser window. It's an essential web browsing technique, but can it be done with the Safari browser?

Yes, indeed. Safari enables you to open a second tab and open the other page in that tab. Even better, all it takes is a quick tap to switch from one tab to the other. And two tabs is just the beginning because Safari allows you to create as many tabs as your surfing needs require.

Note

Rather than opening a page in a new tab, you might prefer to open the page in a separate browser window. The only way to do that is to long press any link, tap Open in New Window, and then use the new browser window to surf to the page you want.

You can use either of the following methods to open a page in a new tab:

⬤ **Tap Safari's New Tab button (+) shown in Figure 4.2.** Safari creates the new tab. You can then select a page from your bookmarks, type the page address, or run a search to find the page you want.

Genius

To customize the New Tab screen, open Settings and then tap Safari. To not show those sites you've surfed to most frequently, tap the Frequently Visited Sites switch to Off. To choose a different set of pages to use as the Favorites, tap Favorites and then tap the folder you want to see. To insert the current page into Safari's Favorites list, tap the Share icon (see Figure 4.2) and then tap Add to Favorites.

⬤ **On a web page, long press a link to display the link options (see Figure 4.1) and then tap Open in New Tab.**

Genius

If you recently closed a tab, you can reopen it quickly by tapping and holding the New Tab button. This displays the Recently Closed Tabs list, which shows the tabs you've closed during the current Safari session. You then tap the tab you want to reopen.

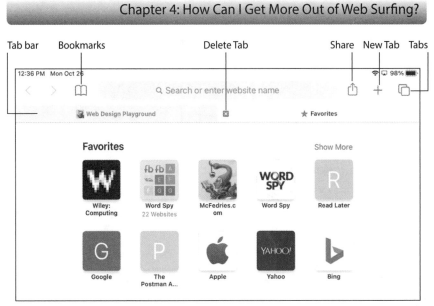

4.2 You can open a new tab by tapping the New Tab button (+) or by tapping and holding a link and then tapping Open in New Tab.

Once you have multiple tabs on the go, you navigate them by tapping the tab you want to view. To close a tab that you no longer need, tap it and then tap the X that appears on the left side of the tab.

Genius

Safari is happy to close old tabs for you automatically. Launch Settings, tap Safari, and then tap Close Tabs. Tap the duration that a tab has been open after which Safari will close the tab for you: After One Day, After One Week, or After One Month.

Opening a tab in the foreground

When you long press a link and then tap Open in Background, Safari creates a new tab and loads the linked page in the tab, but it doesn't switch to that tab. That's often the behavior you want because it lets you finish what you're doing on the current page. However, you might prefer to have Safari load the page in a new tab and immediately switch to that tab, which enables you to check out the linked page right away.

Follow these steps to configure Safari to always open new tabs in the foreground:

1. **On the Home screen, tap Settings.** The Settings app slides in.

2. **Tap Safari.** Your iPad displays the Safari screen.

61

3. **In the Tabs section, tap the Open New Tabs in Background switch to Off, as shown in Figure 4.3.**

TABS

Show Tab Bar

Show Icons in Tabs

Open New Tabs in Background

Close Tabs   Manually >

Allow Safari to automatically close tabs that haven't recently been viewed.

4.3 Tap Open New Tabs in Background to Off to switch to new tabs right away.

With that done, when you now tap and hold a link, you see the Open in New Tab command (instead of Open in Background), which you can tap to open the page and switch to the new tab immediately.

Working with iCloud tabs

Safari tabs in iOS, macOS, or Windows are handy browsing tools because they let you keep multiple websites open and available while you surf other sites. That's fine as long as you use a single device to surf the web, but how realistic is that? It's much more likely that you do some web surfing, not only on your iPad, but also on your Mac or PC and your iPhone. So, what do you do if you're using your tablet to surf and you remember a site that's open in a tab on one of your other devices?

In the past, either you had to wait until you could use the other device again or you could try to find the site on your tablet. Neither is a satisfying solution, so Safari offers a much better idea: iCloud tabs. If you have an iCloud account, you can use it to sync your open Safari tabs with multiple devices and then access those tabs on your iPad. For this to work, you must be using Safari on your other devices, and you must configure iCloud on each device to sync Safari data.

When that's done, open Safari on your tablet and then tap Tabs (pointed out earlier in Figure 4.2). Safari opens the Tabs screen, which displays not only the open tabs on your tablet but also (at the bottom) the open tabs on your other devices.

Viewing a page without distractions

It seems like only a few years ago that purse-lipped pundits and furrow-browed futurologists were lamenting that the Internet signaled the imminent demise of reading. With pursuits such as viral videos and online gaming a mere click or two away, who would ever sit down and actually *read* things? Well, a funny thing happened on the way to the future: People read more now than they ever have. Sure, there's some concern that we're no longer reading long articles and challenging books, but most of us spend much of the day reading online.

On the one hand, this isn't all that surprising because there's just so much text out there, most of it available for free, and much of it professionally written and edited. On the other hand, this is actually quite surprising, because reading an article or essay online is no picnic. The problem is the sheer amount of distractions on almost any page: Background colors or images that clash with the text; ads above, to the side of, and within the text; site features such as search boxes, feed links, and content lists; and those ubiquitous icons for sharing the article with your friends on Facebook, Twitter, Instagram, and on and on.

Fortunately, Safari helps solve this problem by offering the Reader feature. Reader removes all of those extraneous page distractions that get in the way of your reading. So, instead of a hodgepodge of text, icons, and images, you see plain, easy-to-read text. How do you make this happen? By tapping View (pointed out in Figure 4.4) and then tapping Show Reader View. Safari transforms the page to a simpler version, similar to the page shown in Figure 4.5 (the Reader version of the page shown in Figure 4.4). To return to the regular view, tap View and then tap Hide Reader View.

Genius

If you want Safari to automatically display the Reader version of a particular website every time you visit, surf to the site, tap View, tap Website Settings, and then tap the Use Reader Automatically switch to On.

Requesting a website's desktop version

These days, very few websites offer a "mobile" version of the site to iPad users. That's good news because the mobile version almost always offers fewer site features. That's not a compromise you need to make with the iPad's big screen, so if you come across a website that offers up its mobile version, tell the website you want its "desktop" (that is, full-featured) version: Tap View (pointed out later in Figure 4.4) and then tap Request Desktop Website. If you want to return to the mobile version, for some reason, tap View and then tap Request Mobile Website.

Genius

Safari can automatically ask for the desktop version of a particular website. To set this up, surf to the site, tap View, tap Website Settings, and then tap the Request Desktop Website switch to On.

View

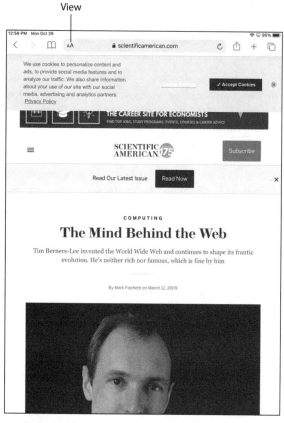

4.4 Today's web pages are often cluttered with elements that get in the way of your reading experience.

Working with bookmarks

The web era is into its fourth decade now (!), so you certainly don't need me to tell you that the web is a manifestly awesome resource that redefines the phrase *treasure trove*. No, at this stage of your web career you're probably most concerned with finding great web treasures and returning to the best or most useful of them in subsequent surfing sessions. The Safari History list can help here (I talk about it later in this chapter), but the best way to ensure that you can easily return to a site a week, a month, or even a year from now is to save it as a bookmark.

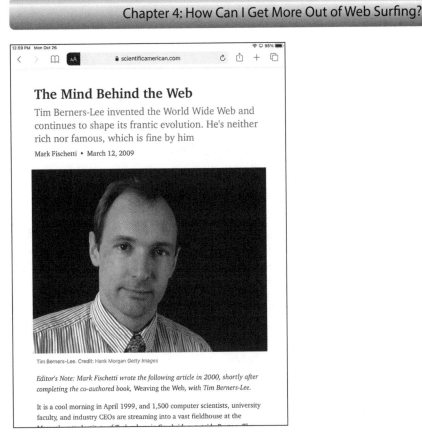

4.5 The Reader version of a web page removes the clutter to focus on the text.

Adding bookmarks

If you think you might want to pay a site another visit down the road, you can follow these steps to create a new bookmark in Safari:

1. **Navigate to the site you want to save.**

2. **Tap Share.** I pointed out this icon in Figure 4.2.

3. **Tap Add Bookmark.** The Add Bookmark dialog appears.

4. **Edit the bookmark name as needed.** This name is what you see when you scroll through your bookmarks.

5. **Tap Location.** This displays a list of your bookmark folders.

6. **Tap the folder you want to use to store the bookmark.**

7. **Tap Save.** Safari saves the bookmark.

65

Surfing to a bookmarked site

After you add a bookmark, how do you use it to return to the site? Like so:

1. **Tap Safari's Bookmarks button (pointed out back in Figure 4.2).**

2. **Tap the Bookmark tab (it looks like an open book).**

3. **If your bookmark resides in a folder, tap the folder.**

4. **Tap the bookmark.** Safari opens the page for you.

Maintaining bookmarks

Once you've added a few bookmarks to Safari's Bookmarks list, most of the time you can forget about them until you need to open the page (as I describe in the previous section). However, your bookmarks might need occasional maintenance such as changing the address, renaming the bookmark, or deleting bookmarks you no longer need.

To perform these and other bookmark maintenance duties, follow these steps to get the Bookmarks list into Edit mode:

1. **Tap the Bookmarks button in the menu bar.** I pointed out this button earlier in Figure 4.2. Safari opens the Bookmarks list.

2. **Tap the Bookmarks tab.** This is the icon that looks like an open book.

3. **If your bookmark resides in a folder, tap the folder.**

4. **Tap Edit.** Your iPad switches the Bookmarks list to Edit mode, and you can use the following techniques:

   - **Edit the bookmark.** Tap the bookmark to open the Edit Bookmark screen; then edit the name, change the address, or choose a different folder. Tap Done when you've completed your edits.

   - **Reorder the bookmarks.** Each bookmark displays a Drag icon on the right. To change where a bookmark appears in the list, drag its icon to the position you prefer.

   - **Create a folder.** Tap New Folder to display the Edit Folder screen, enter a title, and then select a location.

   - **Remove a bookmark.** Tap the Delete button — the white minus (–) sign inside a red circle to the left of the bookmark — and then tap the Delete button that slides in.

Tap Done to exit Edit mode and then tap the Bookmarks icon to close the Bookmarks pane.

Adding pages to your Reading List

In your web travels, you'll often come upon a page with fascinating content that you can't wait to read. Unfortunately, a quick look at the length of the article tells you that you're going to need more time than what you currently have available. What's a body to do? Quickly scan the article and move on with your life? No, when you come across good web content, you need to savor it. So, should you bookmark the article for future reference? That's not bad, but bookmarks are really for things you want to revisit often, not for pages that you might read only once.

The best solution is the Safari feature called the Reading List, which (perhaps not surprisingly) is a simple list of things to read. When you don't have time to read something immediately, store it in your Reading List so you can read it later in your spare time (assuming your busy life allows for such a luxury).

You can use either of the following techniques to add a page to your Reading List:

- Surf to the page you want to read later, tap Share, and then tap Add to Reading List.

- Long press a link for the page that you want to read later and then tap Add to Reading List.

Later, when you have the time (at last!) to read, tap the Bookmarks button, and then tap the Reading List tab (the eyeglasses icon). Safari displays the items that are in your Reading List, and you then tap the item you want to read.

Genius

To make the Reading List a bit easier to navigate, tap Show Unread. This filters the list to display only the pages you haven't read yet.

Revisiting pages using the History list

Bookmarking a website (as I describe earlier in this chapter) is a good idea if that site contains useful or entertaining content that you want to revisit often. Sometimes, however, you may not realize that a site had useful data until a day or two later. Similarly, you may like a site's stuff but decide against bookmarking it, only to regret that decision down the road. You could waste a big chunk of your day trying to track down the site, or you may run into Web Browsing Law #23: A great site that you forget to bookmark can never be located again.

Fortunately, Safari has you covered. As you surf the web, Safari keeps track of each page you visit, storing the name and address of every page in the History list. Here's how to use it:

1. **Tap the Bookmarks button.** Safari opens the Bookmarks list.

2. **Tap the History tab (the clock icon).** Safari opens the History screen, which shows the sites you've visited today at the top, followed by a list of previous surfing dates.

3. **If you visited the site you're looking for on a previous day, tap that day.** Safari displays a list of only the sites you visited on that day.

4. **Tap the site you want to revisit.** Safari loads it.

Dealing with Forms

Many websites offer forms where you fill in some data and then submit the form to a server for processing. Doing this in the Safari browser is pretty straightforward. Use the following techniques to fill in online forms on your iPad:

- **Text box.** Tap inside the text box to bring the touchscreen keyboard on-screen; then tap your text.

- **Text area.** Tap inside the text area and then use the keyboard to tap your text. Most text areas allow multiline entries, so you can tap Return to start a new line.

- **Check box.** Tap the check box to toggle it on and off.

- **Radio button.** Tap the radio button to activate it.

- **Command button.** Tap the button to make it run its command (usually to submit the form).

Many online forms consist of a series of text boxes. The usual way of filling in all the boxes is to tap inside one, tap your text, tap inside the next one, tap your text, and so on until you're done. That's not onerous, but Safari does offer a slightly easier method:

1. **Tap inside the first text box.** The keyboard appears.

2. **Tap to type the text you want to submit.** Above the keyboard, notice the Previous and Next buttons, as pointed out in Figure 4.6.

3. **Tap Next to move to the next text box.** If you need to return to a text box, tap Previous instead.

4. **Repeat Steps 2 and 3 to fill in the text boxes.**

Next

Previous

Name:	Email:
Paolo	Optional

Message:

Send Your Message

4.6 In a form that contains two or more text boxes, use the Previous and Next buttons to navigate them.

Lots of forms offer at least one selection list, and Safari handles them in an interesting way. When you tap a list, Safari displays the list items in a separate box, as shown in Figure 4.7. In the list of items, the currently selected one appears with a check mark next to it. Tap the item that you want to select.

Filling in forms faster with AutoFill

Safari makes it relatively easy to fill in forms, but it can still be a bit of a slog, especially if the form requires lots of text input. To help make your form chores

Putting On Hairs: Reader Survey

Select your hair color:

Brunette

Black

Blonde

Brunette ✓

Red

Something neon

None

4.7 Tap a list to see its items in a separate box for easier selection.

69

less of a burden, Safari offers a feature called AutoFill, which saves the form data you enter and lets you complete similar forms with the tap of a button.

To take advantage of this useful feature, you have to activate it by following these steps:

1. **Tap Settings.** iPadOS opens the Settings app.

2. **Tap Safari.** The Safari settings appear.

3. **Tap AutoFill.** The AutoFill settings appear.

4. **Tap the Use Contact Info switch to On.** This tells Safari to use your Contacts item to fill in your personal data on a form. For example, if a form requires your name, Safari uses your contact name.

5. **Tap My Info and then tap your name in the Contacts list.**

6. **To have Safari save the credit card information you enter when making online purchases, tap the Credit Cards switch to On.**

Genius

iPadOS enables you to capture credit card data automatically using the iPad's camera. In the AutoFill screen, tap Saved Credit Cards, verify your identity (using Face ID, Touch ID, or a passcode), and then tap Add Credit Card. (Let me stress that you definitely need to use one of these security features if you're saving credit cards to your iPad; see Chapter 3.) Tap Use Camera, bring your credit card within the rectangle, and then wait until the card data has been captured.

With AutoFill activated, when you tap inside any text field in an online form, the AutoFill Contact button shows up just above the keyboard. Tap AutoFill Contact and Safari fills in those elements in the form that jibe with your contact data, as shown in Figure 4.8. How do you know which fields will get filled in automatically? Safari adds a colored background to each field (in Figure 4.8, see the First Name and Last Name fields).

Storing website login data

You can also configure Safari's AutoFill feature to remember website usernames and passwords. Follow these steps to activate this feature:

1. **Tap Settings.** iPadOS opens the Settings app.

2. **Tap Passwords.** iPadOS prompts you to identify yourself using Face ID, Touch ID, or a passcode.

3. **Verify your identity.** The Passwords screen appears.

4. **Tap the AutoFill Passwords switch to On.** Note that although the switch name just says "Passwords," this feature actually saves both the password and username for each site.

With the AutoFill Passwords option activated, each time you enter a password to log in to a site for the first time, Safari asks if you want to remember the login data by displaying the dialog shown in Figure 4.9, which offers three choices:

- **Save Password.** Tells Safari to remember the site's username and password.

- **Never for This Website.** Tells Safari not to save the site's username and password and to never prompt you again to save the site's login data.

- **Not Now.** Tells Safari not to remember the site's username and password this time, but to ask you again the next time you log in to this site.

Please tell me about yourself:

First Name: [Paul]

Last Name: [McFedries]

Nickname: [|]

Nom de Plume: [ ]

Nom de Guerre: [ ]

(Just Do It!) (Just Reset It!)

AutoFill Contact

4.8 Tap AutoFill Contact to fill in form fields that correspond to your contact data.

Genius

You can remove any saved password from your iPad. Tap Settings, tap Passwords, and then verify your identity (using Face ID, Touch ID, or a passcode) to see all your saved passwords. Swipe left on the login data you want to remove; then tap the Delete button that appears.

Note

Safari is prudent about saving site login data, meaning that it won't offer to save the data for every site. In particular, when you log in to a secure site — such as an online bank or corporate website — Safari won't ask to save the site's username and password.

After you save a site's username and password, the next time you navigate to the site's login page and tap either the username or password field, Safari displays a Use *"username"* prompt like the one shown near the bottom of the screen in Figure 4.10. Either tap the suggested username or tap the Keychain icon (pointed out in Figure 4.10) to see the site's saved logins and then tap the login you prefer to use. Safari fills in the username and password, so all you do is tap Log In (or Sign In, or whatever).

Storing website logins manually

If a website or your Internet connection is unavailable, you can still save a website's login data manually. You might also want to save two or more sets of login credentials for an existing site, and it's easiest to enter those extra logins manually. Here are the steps to follow:

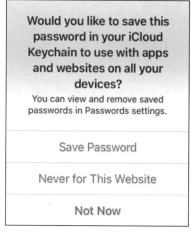

Would you like to save this password in your iCloud Keychain to use with apps and websites on all your devices?

You can view and remove saved passwords in Passwords settings.

Save Password

Never for This Website

Not Now

4.9 If you set up Safari to save passwords, you see this dialog when you log in to a site.

1. **Open the Settings app.**

2. **Tap Passwords.** iPadOS prompts you to identify yourself using Face ID, Touch ID, or a passcode.

Caution

Strangely, the text you enter into the Password field doesn't appear as dots, as you might expect, but as plain text. Therefore, make sure there's no one around who can view the password text as you enter it.

3. **Verify your identity.** The Passwords screen appears.

4. **Tap Add Password (+) at the top of the screen.** The Add Password dialog appears.

5. **Enter the website's address as well as your login credentials — username and password — for the site.**

6. **Tap Done.** Settings adds the login information for the site.

Keychain

4.10 Safari asks if it you want to use a site's saved login data the next time you attempt to log in to the site.

Enhancing Web Browsing Privacy

Safari stores a ton of data related to your web browsing, so it pays to take some time to manage that data as a way of enhancing your online privacy. The next few sections show you how it's done.

Deleting sites from your browsing history

Whenever I mention deleting sites from the browser's history, everyone thinks I'm talking about sites that could cause embarrassment if discovered (I'm sure you can guess what types of sites I'm talking about). Well, that's true, but it's not the only reason why you might want to prune sites from Safari's History list. Here are a few more:

- You visit a site that you prefer to keep private, such as a financial site or a corporate site.

73

- You tap what appears to be a legitimate link (in, say, an email), only to end up on some unsavory website.

- You don't like the idea of Safari tracking your movements.

Whatever the reason, follow these steps to wipe out some or all of your Safari browsing history:

1. **Tap the Bookmarks button.** Safari opens the Bookmarks list.

2. **Tap the History tab (the clock icon).** Safari opens the History pane.

3. **Tap Clear.** Safari asks how much of your history you want to delete.

4. **Tap a time period: The Last Hour, Today, Today and Yesterday, or All Time.** Safari removes every site from the History list for the time period you selected.

Genius

There's another way to clear the History, and it may be faster if you're not currently working in Safari. Open Settings, tap Safari, and then tap Clear History and Website Data. When Settings ask you to confirm, tap Clear.

Removing website data

During your web browsing session, Safari stores quite a bit of information for each website. This information includes the following:

- Some site text and images, which enables Safari to load the page faster when you revisit the site the next time.

- AutoFill data for form fields and site login credentials.

- Small text files called *cookies* that save data for things like shopping carts, site settings, and your site preferences.

Storing all this data can speed up your surfing, but it's not always safe or private. If, say, you have Safari save a site password, that could be a problem if other people share your iPad. And those site cookies aren't always benign because they're sometimes used to track your online activities.

To delete the data that Safari stores for a website, follow these steps:

1. **Open Settings.**

2. **Tap Safari.** The Safari settings appear.

3. **Tap Advanced.** The Advanced settings appear.

4. **Tap Website Data.** Settings displays a list of the recent sites for which Safari has stored data. The list shows both the site domain name and the size of the saved data.

5. **If the site you want to delete doesn't appear on the initial list, tap Show All Sites.** Settings displays the complete list of sites.

6. **Tap Edit.**

7. **Tap the red Delete icon to the left of the site you want to clear.**

8. **Tap the Delete button that appears to the right of the site's data size value.** Safari removes the site's data.

Genius

If you're selling your iPad, it's a good idea to clean house by removing *all* the website data stored by Safari. At the bottom of the Website Data screen, tap Remove All Website Data. When Settings asks you to confirm, tap Remove.

Browsing privately

Rather than deleting your browsing history or website data manually, you can save yourself a lot of time by asking Safari to not save any of that data for a little while. You do this by using a feature called *private browsing*, which means that Safari doesn't save any of the following data as you browse:

- Your browsing history

- Web page text and images

- Search text you enter into the address bar

- Website cookies

- AutoFill usernames and passwords

To surf under the protection of private browsing, follow these steps:

1. **Tap the Tabs button.**

2. **Tap Private.** Safari creates a separate set of tabs dedicated to private browsing.

3. **Tap Add Tab (+).** Safari creates a new private tab.

Genius

Safari can compromise your privacy by showing suggestions while you're typing search text into the address bar. If someone is peeping over your shoulder or if you lend your iPad to someone to do a quick Safari search, she might see these suggestions. To prevent Safari from showing suggestions, open the Settings app and tap Safari; tap the Search Engine Suggestions switch to Off; and then tap the Safari Suggestions switch to Off.

Making Safari Even Easier and Better

The rest of this chapter takes you through a few useful techniques that can make Safari even easier to use.

Switching the default search engine

Safari's default search engine is Google. Nothing wrong with that, of course, but if you prefer a different search engine, follow these steps to change it:

1. **Open Settings.**

2. **Tap Safari.** The Safari settings appear.

3. **Tap Search Engine.** The Search Engine settings appear.

4. **Tap the search engine you want to use.** You have three choices besides Google: Yahoo, Bing, or DuckDuckGo.

Searching for text in a web page

If you surf to a web page to look for specific information, you could scroll the page to find what you want, but it's almost always easier to search for the data you're looking for. Here's how:

1. **Surf to the page that contains the information you want.**

2. **Tap the Share icon.**

3. **Tap Find on Page.** Safari displays the search text box.

4. **Type the search text you want to use.** Safari highlights the first instance of the search text, as shown in Figure 4.11.

4.11 Safari highlights the first usage of your search text.

5. **Tap the down-pointing arrow to cycle forward through the instances of the search term that appear on the page.** You can also cycle backward through the results by tapping the up-pointing arrow.

6. **When you're finished with the search, tap Done.**

Searching the web with Siri

If you like asking Siri for information, then you'll love the fact that Siri can also do web searches. Here are some tips to bear in mind when web searching with Siri voice commands:

- **Searching the entire web.** Say "Search the web for *topic*," where *topic* is your search criteria.

- **Searching Wikipedia.** Say "Search Wikipedia for *topic*," where *topic* is the subject you want to look up.

◉ **Searching with a particular search engine.** Say "Use *Engine* to search for *topic*," where *Engine* is the name of the search engine, such as Google or Bing, and *topic* is your search criteria.

Siri also understands commands related to searching for businesses and restaurants through its partnership with Yelp. To look for businesses and restaurants using Siri, the general syntax to use is the following (although, as usual with Siri, you don't have to be too rigid about this):

"Find (or Look for) *something somewhere*."

Here, the *something* part can be the name of a business (such as "Starbucks"), a type of business (such as "gas station"), a type of restaurant (such as "Thai restaurants"), or a generic product (such as "coffee"). The *somewhere* part can be something relative to your current location (such as "around here" or "near me" or "within walking distance") or a specific location (such as "in Indianapolis" or "in Broad Ripple"). Here are some examples:

◉ "Find a gas station within walking distance."

◉ "Look for pizza restaurants in Indianapolis."

◉ "Find coffee around here."

◉ "Look for a grocery store near me."

Note, too, that if you add a qualifier such as "good" or "best" before the *something* portion of the command, Siri returns the results organized by their Yelp rating.

Sharing a link via AirDrop

If you come across a web page that you want someone nearby to check out on that person's device, how do you get the page address from your iPad to that device? You can take advantage of AirDrop, a Bluetooth service that enables two nearby devices — specifically, an iPad, an iPhone, or a Mac — to exchange data wirelessly. Here's how it works with a web page address:

1. **Surf to the web page you want to share.**

2. **Tap the Share icon.**

3. **Tap AirDrop.** The AirDrop screen appears and shows an icon for each nearby device.

4. **Tap the icon for the person with whom you want to share the link.** The other person sees a confirmation dialog. When she taps Accept, her version of Safari (or her default browser) loads and displays the page.

How Do I Make the Most of Email?

With more and more people texting and tweeting, Facetiming and Zooming, the more old-fashioned email seems. Yes, reading and composing email is dishwater dull, but do you know what else it is? It's *universal*. Almost everyone who's online has an email account, and it remains the best way to get in touch and exchange information (at least digitally). Your iPad comes with Mail, a decent email app that's easy to use, but there are still plenty of tricks and techniques you should know to help you get the most out of Mail on your tablet.

Managing Your Accounts

The Mail app is a nice email program that makes the most of the two iPad orientations. In portrait mode, you see a big version of the current message, complete with embedded photos and other media. In landscape mode, you get a two-pane view with your Inbox messages in one pane and the current message in the other. Landscape mode is great for composing messages because you get the larger keyboard and a nice, big compose window.

Mail also has a raft of settings and features that make it ideal for doing the email thing while you're away from your desk. Before getting to all that, you need to configure your tablet with an email account or two.

Adding an email account manually

How you add an email account to your iPad depends on which service or type of account you want to add. For email services, iPadOS can work with the following:

- **iCloud**
- **Microsoft Exchange**
- **Google (that is, Gmail)**
- **Yahoo!**
- **AOL**
- **Outlook.com**

Note

For most of these email services, when you add the account to your iPad, you're adding not only the service's email component, but also the service's calendars and contacts (and perhaps other services, such as notes).You can turn off these components if you don't want to use them: Open Settings, tap Mail, tap Accounts, tap the service, and then turn off the switch for each component you don't want to use.

iPadOS can configure these services for you automatically when you provide your account address and password.

iPadOS also supports these account types:

- **POP (Post Office Protocol)**
- **IMAP (Internet Message Access Protocol)**

The details behind these account types aren't important. All you need to know is which type applies to your account and the details of your account, which will include some or all of the following:

- The account email address

- The account username (which is often the account email address) and password

- The host name of the email service's incoming mail server

- The host name of the email service's outgoing mail server

- The security settings that you need to specify to receive and send messages

Before proceeding with the setup of a POP or IMAP account, make sure you have the required information, which you can get either from your network administrator or from your email provider's support web pages.

Here are the steps to follow to add a new account to your iPad:

1. **Open Settings.**

2. **Tap Mail.** iPadOS opens the Mail settings.

3. **Tap Accounts.** The Accounts settings appear.

4. **Tap Add Account.** The Add Account dialog appears, as shown in Figure 5.1.

5.1   Use the Add Account dialog to select the service you want to set up.

5. **Do one of the following:**

- **To set up an iCloud, Exchange, Google (Gmail), Yahoo!, AOL, or Outlook.com account, tap the logo.** Type your name, the account email address and password, and a description of the account; then tap Next. Leave the Mail switch On, turn on any other components you want to use (such as Calendars or Contacts), and then tap Save. You're done, so you can skip the rest of these steps. Sweet!

- **If you're adding a POP or IMAP account, tap Other and procced to Step 6.**

6. **Tap Add Mail Account.** The New Account dialog appears.

7. **Type your name, type the account's email address and password, type a description, and then tap Next.**

8. **Tap the tab that corresponds to the type of email account you're setting up: IMAP or POP.**

9. **For the account's incoming mail server, type the host name and your account username and password.**

10. **For the account's outgoing mail server, type the host name and your account username and password.**

11. **Tap Save.** iPadOS verifies the account. When that's done, you're returned to the Accounts screen, where your new account now appears.

Changing the default account

iPadOS sets up a default account, which is the account that Mail uses when you send any message (which could be a new message, a reply to a message, or a forwarded message). If you have only one account on your iPad, that account is automatically the default. However, if you've set up multiple accounts, then you might want to change the default, which you can do by following these steps:

1. **Open the Settings app.**

2. **Tap Mail.** iPadOS opens the Mail settings.

3. **Tap Default Account.** The Default Account screen appears.

4. **Tap an account.** Mail will now use that account as the default for sending messages.

Disabling an account

If you don't want Mail to check an account for new messages (for example, your battery is running low and you're trying to save resources), you can temporarily disable the account's Mail component as follows:

1. **Open the Settings app.**

2. **Tap Mail.** iPadOS opens the Mail settings.

3. **Tap Accounts.** The Accounts settings appear.

4. **Tap the account.** iPadOS displays the account's settings.

5. **Do one of the following:**

   • **If you're working with a POP account, tap the Account switch to Off.**

   • **For all other account types, tap the Mail switch to Off,**

   as shown in Figure 5.2. Feel free to also disable other account data types, such as contacts and calendars, as needed.

GMAIL	
Account	pmcfedries@gmail.com >
Mail	
Contacts	
Calendars	
Notes	
Delete Account	

5.2 For most account types, you temporarily disable email checks by tapping the Mail switch to Off.

To enable mail on the account, repeat Steps 1 to 5 to set the Account switch (for a POP account) or the Mail switch (for all other accounts) back to On.

Removing an account

If you no longer use an account, you should delete it by following these steps:

1. **Open the Settings app.**

2. **Tap Mail.** iPadOS opens the Mail settings.

3. **Tap Accounts.** iPadOS opens the Accounts settings.

4. **Tap the account.** iPadOS opens the account's settings.

5. **Tap Delete Account.** iPadOS asks you to confirm.

6. **Tap Delete Account.** iPadOS returns you to the Accounts screen, which no longer displays the deleted account.

Switching from one account to another

If you've added two or more accounts to your iPad, follow these steps in the Mail app to switch from one account to another:

1. **In Mail, tap the Back button (<) until you see the Mailboxes pane, as shown in Figure 5.3.**

2. **Tap the account you want to view:**

   - **To work with just the account's Inbox, tap the account name as it appears under the All Inboxes folder.**

   - **To work with all the account's folders, tap the bold version of the account name in the Mailboxes pane.** This opens a list of all the account's available folders. Now tap the folder you want to view.

Edit

Mailboxes

✉ All Inboxes		52
✉ iCloud		44
✉ POP Account		4
✉ Gmail		4
☆ VIP		
⚑ Flagged		
✉ Unread		52
iCloud		44 >
POP Account		⌄
✉ Inbox		4
Gmail		⌄
✉ Inbox		4
◻ Drafts		
◁ Sent		6
⌧ Junk		7
🗑 Trash		12

5.3 Use the Mailboxes pane to choose the other account.

Genius

To customize what you see in the Mailboxes pane, tap Edit, tap to activate the check box beside each folder you want to add to the Mailboxes pane (or tap to deactivate the check box beside each folder you want to remove from the Mailboxes pane), and then tap Done.

Configuring Some Useful Mail Settings

This section shows you how to modify a few useful Mail settings to make your email chores a bit easier.

Creating a custom email signature

A *signature* is a bit of text that appears at the end of your messages. Most signatures include the sender's name and perhaps a short signoff, but they can also include contact information, a favorite quotation, and whatever else you want people to know about you. The Mail app ignores all of this and inserts the following signature to your new messages, as well as to your replies and forwards:

```
Sent from my iPad
```

It's likely your recipients don't need (or, to be honest, care) to know which device you're using, so you'll want to create a custom signature that's more informative and unique. Here's how it's done:

1. **Open the Settings app.**

2. **Tap Mail.** iPadOS opens the Mail settings.

3. **Tap Signature.** iPadOS opens the Signature screen.

4. **Select one of the following:**

   - **All Accounts.** You create one custom signature, and Mail uses it for all your iPad accounts.

   - **Per Account.** You create a custom signature for each of your iPad accounts.

5. **Specify your custom signature or signatures as follows:**

   - If you selected All Accounts in Step 4, tap the default signature and then enter your custom signature.

   - If you selected Per Account in Step 4, then for each of your iPad accounts, tap the account's signature and then enter your custom signature for the account.

Thwarting spammers by disabling remote images

A *web bug* is an image that's stored on a server and is added to an email message not by inserting the image directly, but by referencing the image's address on the server. When you open the message, Mail uses that server address to download the image and display it in the message.

There's nothing wrong with any of this per se, but spammers often use web bugs as a way of checking to see if an email address is valid (active email addresses are like gold to your average junk mail operator). They do that by configuring the web bug's server address to also include either your email address directly or some kind of code that references your address. This means that when the server gets a request for the image, a program on the server also notes your email address as valid.

That's bad news, indeed, because it just means you'll end up getting even more spam than you already do. To prevent this, you need to configure Mail to not load remote images when it opens an email message:

1. **Open the Settings app.**

2. **Tap Mail.** iPadOS displays the Mail settings.

3. **Tap Load Remote Images to turn that switch Off.** Mail no longer downloads remote images to your email messages.

Stopping messages from getting organized by thread

In Mail, a *thread* is the collection of messages that consists of the original message and all of its replies. By default, Mail organizes your messages by thread, which means that all of a thread's messages appear as a single item in the account's Inbox. To indicate a thread, Mail displays a circled arrow (>), as shown in Figure 5.4. Tapping the thread displays a list of the messages in the thread, and you can then tap whatever thread message you want to read.

A circled arrow indicates a message thread

2:50 PM Wed Oct 28

‹ iCloud   **Inbox**   Edit

● **Apple Developer**   9/15/20
Get your next generation app ready.
Submit your apps to the App Store App
Store Connect is now accepting apps built...

Paul McFedries   9/10/20 ⊙
Check out my latest iPhone photos
I've been busy with my new iPhone, so
check out my latest here:

5.4 A circled arrow on the right side of a message indicates a thread.

Organizing related messages into a single thread helps to keep your Inbox neat, and it usually makes it easier to find a particular thread message. However, if you routinely deal with short threads (say, two or three messages max), then it's almost always easier to find the message you want if they're not grouped into threads. Fortunately, in this case you can turn off threads by following these steps:

1. **Open the Settings app.**

2. **Tap Mail.** iPadOS displays the Mail settings.

3. **Tap Organize by Thread to turn that switch Off.** Mail no longer organizes your messages by thread.

Customizing Mail's swipe options

A bit later in this chapter I show you how to maintain messages in Mail by using swipe gestures. You can also customize which tasks Mail displays when you swipe a message:

1. **Open the Settings app.**

2. **Tap Mail.** iPadOS displays the Mail settings.

3. **Tap Swipe Options.** iPadOS opens the Swipe Options screen.

4. **Tap Swipe Left and then tap the action you want Mail to present when you swipe left on a message.** Tap Back (<) to return to the previous screen.

5. **Tap Swipe Right and then tap the action you want Mail to present when you swipe right on a message.**

Working with Email Messages

The rest of this chapter takes you through a few useful and timesaving Mail app techniques for handling email on your iPad.

Adding iCloud folders

Any folders (Apple actually calls them mailboxes) that you create on your iCloud account are automatically mirrored in the Mail app on your iPad. You could go to the iCloud website to create new folders, but the Mail app enables you to add new ones right from your iPad. Here are the steps to follow:

1. **In Mail, tap Back (<) until you get to the Mailboxes pane.**

2. **Tap Edit.** Mail displays the iCloud folders list.

3. **Tap New Mailbox.**

4. **Enter a name for the new folder.**

5. **Tap Mailbox Location.**

6. **Tap the existing iCloud folder that you want to use to store your new folder.** To create a new top-level folder instead, tap iCloud.

7. **Tap Save.** Mail adds the folder to iCloud.

8. **Tap Done.**

Note

> To move an email message to your new iCloud folder, open the iCloud Inbox, tap the message, tap Move (it's the folder icon), and then tap your new folder.

Attaching a document from iCloud Drive

If you have documents stored in iCloud Drive and you want to share one of those documents via email, you can send the document directly from iCloud Drive as a file attachment:

1. **In Mail, create a new message.**
2. **Tap an empty area of the message body.** Mail displays a toolbar.
3. **Tap Document.** This is the icon that looks like a document.
4. **Tap Add Document.** Mail displays the iCloud Drive screen.
5. **Locate and then tap the document you want to send.** Mail attaches the file to your email.

Formatting message text

If you want to spruce up your email text, Mail offers a Format dialog that includes formatting options such as bold, italics, and underline; typography options such as the typeface, font size, and text color; bulleted and numbered lists; alignment settings; and more. Here are the steps to follow to format message text in Mail:

1. **In your message, tap anywhere within the word or phrase you want to work with.** Mail displays the cursor.
2. **Tap the cursor.** Mail displays some text options.
3. **Tap Select.** Mail selects the word that includes or is closest to the cursor.
4. **(Optional) Drag the selection handles to select all the text you want to format.**
5. **Tap the Format (Aa) button in the toolbar.** Mail displays the Format dialog, as shown in Figure 5.5.
6. **Use the controls in the Format dialog to format the selected text.**
7. **Tap outside of the Format dialog to close it.**

Format

5.5 You can use the Format dialog to apply a wide range of formatting to the selected text.

To store your current message as a draft that you can work on later, tap Cancel and then tap Save Draft. To reopen the message later, open the account in the Mailboxes pane, tap Drafts, and then tap your draft message.

Maintaining messages with swipe gestures

Mail can help speed you through a long list of messages to process by offering swipe gestures to perform a few message maintenance chores. Here are the maintenance tasks you can perform using gestures:

- **Mark a message as read.** Either swipe right on the message and then tap Read (see Figure 5.6), or drag the message to the right until the Unread icon (the blue dot) disappears.

5.6 Swipe right on a message to mark it as read.

- **Flag a message.** Swipe left on the message and then tap Flag (see Figure 5.7).

5.7 Swipe left on a message to flag it.

- **Reply, Reply All, Forward, Trash, Flag, Mark as Read (or Mark as Unread), Move Message, Archive Message, Move to Junk, Mute, or Notify Me.** Swipe left on the message, tap More, and then tap one of these commands from the menu that appears.

- **Delete a message.** Either swipe left on the message and then tap Trash or drag the message to the left until it disappears from the Inbox.

Marking every message as read

In the previous section, I show you that you can mark a message as read by swiping right on it and then tapping Read. This is quick and easy for a small number of messages, but slow and cumbersome for a large number of messages. Fortunately, Mail lets you perform the following steps to mark *every* message in the current mailbox as read:

1. **Open the mailbox that contains the messages you want to mark.**

2. **Tap Edit.** Mail displays the mailbox editing tools.

3. **Tap Select All.** Mail selects every message.

4. **Tap Mark.** Mail asks how you want the messages marked.

5. **Tap Mark as Read.** Mail marks every message as having been read.

Controlling email with Siri voice commands

You can use the Siri voice recognition app to check, compose, send, and reply to messages, all with simple voice commands. Tap and hold the Home button (or press and hold the Mic button of the iPad headphones, or the equivalent button on a Bluetooth headset) until Siri appears.

To check for new email messages on your iCloud account, you need only say "Check email" (or just "Check mail"). You can also view a list of iCloud messages as follows:

- **Displaying unread messages.** Say "Show new email."

- **Displaying messages where the subject line contains a specified topic.** Say "Show email about *topic*," where *topic* is the topic you want to view.

- **Displaying messages from a particular person.** Say "Show email from *name*," where *name* is the name of the sender.

To start a new email message, Siri gives you a couple of options:

● **Creating a new message addressed to a particular person.** Say "Email *name*," where *name* is the name of the recipient. This name can be a name from your Contacts list or someone with a defined relationship, such as "Mom" or "my brother."

● **Creating a new message with a particular subject line.** Say "Email *name* about *subject*," where *name* defines the recipient, and *subject* is the subject line text.

In each case, Siri creates the new message, displays it, and then asks if you want to send it. If you do, you can either say "Send" or tap the Send button.

If you have a message displayed, you can send a response by saying "Reply." If you want to add some text to the response, say "Reply *text*," where *text* is your response.

You can also use Siri within Mail to dictate a message. When you tap inside the body of a new message, the keyboard that appears shows a Mic icon beside the spacebar. Tap the Mic icon and then start dictating. Here are some notes:

● For punctuation, you can say the name of the mark you need, such as "comma" (,), "semicolon" (;), "colon" (:), "period" or "full stop" (.), "question mark" (?), "exclamation point" (!), "dash" (–), or "at sign" (@).

● You can enclose text in parentheses by saying "open parenthesis," then the text, and then "close parenthesis."

● To surround text with quotation marks, say "open quote," then the text, and then "close quote."

● To render a word in all uppercase letters, say "all caps" and then say the word.

● To start a new paragraph, say "new line."

● You can have some fun by saying "smiley face" for :-), "winky face" for ;-), and "frowny face" for :-(.

● To spell out a word (such as "period" or "colon"), say "No caps on, no space on," spell the word, and then say "No space off, no caps off."

When you're finished, tap Done.

93

How Can I Have Fun with Photos?

The sharp display on the iPad makes it the perfect portable photo album. No more whipping out wallet shots of your kids — just show people your on-screen photo albums. The iPad also comes with some great features that make it a breeze to browse photos and run slide shows. However, your tablet is capable of more than just viewing photos. It's actually loaded with cool features that enable you to manipulate and take photos and to use your images to enhance other parts of your digital life. This chapter is your guide to these features.

Browsing and Viewing Your Photos

Your iPad offers lots of features for working with photos, and you'll find most of those features in an app called Photos. When you launch Photos, the app starts you off in the All Photos tab (see Figure 6.1), which displays your photos, arranged by the date each was taken, with the newest photos at the bottom. You can also organize the photos by date by tapping one of the other tabs: Years, Months, or Days. For example, if you tap Months, you see headings for each month along with a sample image from that month — tap the heading or the image to see that month's photos and then tap the photo you want to view.

Genius

One quirk of the All Photos tab is that it shows every photo as a square, which means Photos temporarily crops each photo to make it fit. If you prefer to have your photos displayed uncropped so that you can see them in their original portrait or landscape aspect ratio, tap the Aspect button.

6.1 The All Photos tab shows — you guessed it! — all your photos.

Navigating and manipulating photos

You can do so much with your photos after they're on your iPad, and it isn't your normal photo-browsing experience. You aren't just a passive viewer because you can actually take some control over what you see and how the pictures are presented:

- **Scrolling through your photos.** Once you have an individual photo on-screen, you view more photos by flicking left to view the next photo or flicking right to view the previous image. Alternatively, tap the screen to display a sequence of thumbnails at the bottom of the Photos app window and run your finger along those thumbnails to quickly peruse the photos.

- **Rotating the screen for the best view.** If you have your iPad in portrait orientation and you're viewing a photo that was taken in landscape mode, the Photos app scales down the photo so that its fits the width of the screen and displays white space above and below the photo. Nothing wrong with that, but you can get the best view of the photo by rotating the screen into landscape orientation. The photo rotates, too, but now it satisfyingly fills the whole screen. Rotate the tablet back to portrait orientation when the next photo taken in portrait mode shows up.

- **Flipping the iPad.** To show a photo to another person, flip the iPad so that the back is toward you and the bottom is now the top. The Photos app automatically flips the photo right-side up.

- **Zooming in and out of a photo.** If there's a portion of a photo you want to get a closer look at, you can zoom in to magnify the shot. You can do this in either of the following ways:

  - **Double-tap.** To zoom in, double-tap the spot on the photo you want to magnify. Photos dutifully doubles the size of the place where you tapped. Double-tap anywhere on the screen to return to the original magnification.

  - **Spread and pinch.** To zoom in, spread two fingers apart over the spot you want to magnify. To return to the original magnification, pinch two fingers together anywhere on the screen.

- **Panning a photo.** After you zoom in on a photo, drag your finger on the screen to move — or *pan* — the photo along with your finger.

Note

When you're zoomed in on a photo, it's best to reset the magnification before resuming your photo scrolling. Why? Because while you're zoomed in, Photos interprets left and right flicks as panning gestures, not scrolling gestures. You can still get to the next photo, but it takes a lot more work.

Creating a photo album

If you have been taking a lot of pictures on your iPad, the Photos app enables you to create your own photo albums right on your device, which is a handy way to organize your shots. Follow these steps to create a photo album:

1. **In the Photos app, tap Back (<) until you see the Photos pane.**

2. **At the bottom of the Photos pane, tap New Album.** Photos prompts you for an album name.

3. **Type the album name, and then tap Save.** Photos displays a list of your tablet images.

4. **Tap each image that you want to include in your new album.** Photos adds a check mark to each selected photo.

5. **Tap Done.** Photos creates the new album and adds it to the My Albums section of the Photos pane.

Note

To delete an album you no longer use (but keep the photos on your iPad), display the Photos pane, tap Edit, tap the red Delete button to the left of the album, and then tap the Delete button that appears. Photos, still not convinced you mean it, asks you to confirm: Tap Delete Album to finally make it happen.

Marking a photo as a favorite

If you take a lot of photos with your iPad, not all of them will be gems, but *some* of them will be. That's great, but the problem is that you have to scroll through a ton of not-so-gemlike images to see your favorites. I know you don't have time for that, so what's the solution? Tell your iPad which of your photos are your favorite ones! The Photos app maintains an album named Favorites that stores these keepers, so you can access your greatest hits with just a few taps.

To mark a photo as a favorite, display it in Photos and then tap the Favorite button (the heart icon).

Streaming photos to Apple TV

If you have an Apple TV that supports AirPlay, you can use AirPlay to stream your photos or a photo slide show from your tablet to your TV.

Follow these steps to stream photos to Apple TV:

1. **Make sure your Apple TV is turned on.**

2. **Using the Photos app, display the album that you want to stream.**

3. **Open the first photo you want to stream.**

4. **Swipe down from the top right corner of the screen.** The Control Center appears.

5. **Tap the Screen Mirroring button.** iPadOS displays a menu of output choices, as shown in Figure 6.2.

6. **Tap the name of your Apple TV device.** The Photos app streams the photo to that device and, hence, to your TV.

6.2 In the Control Center, tap the Screen Mirroring button and then tap your Apple TV device.

Editing a Photo

The iPad isn't the easiest device in the world to use as a camera — it's a bit too big and unwieldy to hold steady. As a result, you might end up with a few less-than-perfect shots. There's not much you can do to fix blurry images (the biggest iPad photo faux pas), but other problems can be fixed by enhancing the color or brightness, cropping out extraneous elements, and applying a filter.

Enhancing color and brightness

If a photo's colors looked washed out or if a photo has areas that are either too dark or too light (or both!), Photos offers an Auto Enhance tool that can automatically adjust for these and other color and brightness problems. Follow these steps to use the Auto Enhance tool:

1. **Open the photo you want to enhance.**

2. **Tap the photo to display the controls.**

3. **Tap Edit.** Photos displays its editing tools.

4. **Tap Enhance (the magic wand icon).** Photos makes an initial adjustment to the color and brightness.

99

5. **Drag the ruler up and down until the photo looks good to you.** As you drag the ruler, Auto Enhance adjusts the color and brightness.

6. **Tap Done.** Photos saves your changes.

Cropping and straightening a photo

Cropping a photo means that you specify a rectangular area of the shot that you want to keep, and everything outside that area is discarded. Why would you do that? Because cropping enables you to get rid of unwanted elements that appear near the edges of the shot, such as a telephone pole, a piece of garbage, or a glimpse of your finger. Even if your photo contains no such extraneous elements, cropping enables you to give center stage to the subject of a photo.

Straightening a photo means that you rotate the shot either clockwise or counterclockwise — we're usually talking just a few degrees here — so that the subject of the photo is level.

Genius

Yep, it's hard to take consistently straight photos with an iPad. A tool that can help with this is the Camera grid, which is a 3 x 3 grid that's superimposed on the Camera screen (the grid doesn't show up in your photos). You can use the horizontal lines of the grid to keep your photos straight. To activate the grid, launch the Settings app, tap Camera, and then tap the Grid switch to On.

Here are the steps to follow to crop and straighten a photo using the Photos app:

1. **Open the photo that you want to edit.**

2. **Tap the photo to display the controls.**

3. **Tap Edit.** Photos displays its editing tools.

4. **Tap Crop (pointed out in Figure 6.3).** Photos displays its tools for cropping and straightening, as shown in Figure 6.3.

5. **To crop the photo, drag one or more corners of the rectangle that appears around your photo.** The idea here is that Photos will retain only that portion of the photo that appears within the rectangle, so drag the corners as needed to set the area you want to keep.

6. **To straighten the photo, tap the Straighten tool and then drag the ruler up or down until the image is level.** You're unlikely to need them, but Photos also offers the Tilt Vertical and Tilt Horizontal tools (pointed out in Figure 6.3) that you can use to tilt your photo vertically or horizontally, respectively. If you feel like it, you can also tap Flip Vertical (pointed out in Figure 6.3) to flip the photo along its vertical axis.

7. **Tap Done.** Photos applies the changes to the photo.

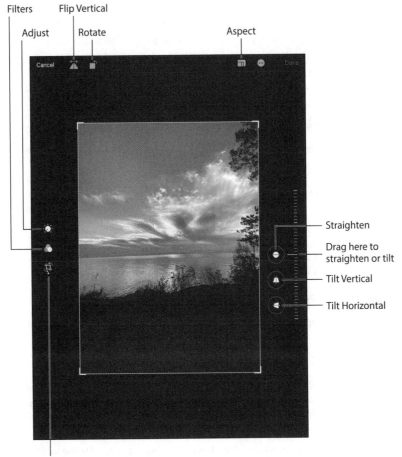

6.3 The Photos app's cropping and straightening tools.

Genius

You can get Photos to do some (or even all) of the cropping work for you by tapping Aspect (pointed out in Figure 6.3) and then tapping a preset aspect ratio, such as Square, 9:16, or 5:7. You then optionally drag the photo so the portion you want to keep is within the crop.

Note

One annoying photo problem is when the photo displays in landscape mode when your tablet is in portrait orientation (or the photo might display in portrait mode when your tablet is in landscape orientation). The solution is to tap the Rotate icon (pointed out in Figure 6.3) to rotate the photo 90 degrees from, say, portrait to landscape.

Applying a filter to a photo

A *filter* is a special effect applied to a photo's colors to give it a different feel. Follow these steps to apply a filter to an image using the Photos app:

1. **Open the photo you want to edit and then tap the photo to display the controls.**

2. **Tap Edit.** Photos displays its editing tools.

3. **Tap Filters (pointed out in Figure 6.3).** Photos displays thumbnail versions of the photo that demonstrate each filter.

4. **Tap the filter you want to use.**

5. **Tap Done.** Photos applies the filter to the photo.

Adjusting the lighting in a photo

Even if you take quite a bit of care setting up and taking your shot, you might still end up with a photo that has poor overall contrast, is underexposed or overexposed, has highlights that are too bright, or has shadows that are too dark. For these and many other lighting issues, Photos offers an impressive array of editing tools that you can use to fiddle with the lighting. Fortunately, you don't have to know how most of these tools work because for the vast majority of photos, you can usually get the lighting just right by working with the following four tools:

- **Contrast.** Use this tool to fix the distribution of the tones (the light and dark areas) in your photo. If the photo's tones are quite different (which can be distracting), try lowering the contrast to make the tones more similar; if the photo's tones are quite similar (which can make a photo look bland), try increasing the contrast to make the tones more different.

- **Exposure.** Use this tool to fix the overall lighting in your photo. If your photo is too light (so it looks washed out), try decreasing the exposure to darken the photo; if your photo is too dark (so it looks muddy), try increasing the exposure to lighten the photo.

- **Highlights.** Use this tool to fix the intensity of the brightest parts of your photo. If your photo has areas that are too bright (and so they look washed out), you can usually fix that by reducing the Highlights value.

- **Shadows.** Use this tool to fix the intensity of the darkest parts of your photo. If your photo has areas that are too dark (and so they show no detail), you can usually repair that problem by reducing the Shadows value.

Here are the steps to follow:

1. **Open the photo you want to adjust and tap the photo to display the controls.**

2. **Tap Edit.** Photos displays its editing tools.

3. **Tap Adjust (pointed out in Figure 6.3).** Photos displays the lighting adjustment controls.

4. **Tap the control you want to use and then drag the ruler to adjust the lighting.**

5. **Repeat Step 4 for each lighting adjustment you want to apply.**

6. **Tap Done.** Photos applies the lighting adjustments to the photo.

Using the Cameras

Your iPad comes with two digital cameras that you can use to take photos. The rest of this chapter explores these cameras and what you can do with them. (This chapter focuses on using the cameras to take photos; if you're interested in video, see Chapter 7.)

Launching the Camera app

As you soon see (in the next section), taking a photo on your iPad requires just a few steps. However, before that can happen you need to get the Camera app on-screen. There are three methods you can use:

- On the Home screen, tap the Camera icon.
- Display the Control Center and then tap the Camera icon.
- From the Lock screen, swipe left.

The first time you run the Camera app, it asks permission to use your current location. Why would Camera need such info? Because Camera supports *geotagging*, which embeds location information into each photo, which enables you to view your photos by location or to map your photos. These are useful features, so when Camera asks if it can use your location, be sure to tap Allow.

Note

To view your photo locations, run the Photos app, tap Back (<) until you see the Photos pane, and then tap Places. In the screen that appears, tap the Map tab to see your locations on a map, or tap the Grid tab to see a list of your locations.

Caution

Geotagging makes it easy to map your photos, but it also raises privacy issues because it means that each photo comes with its location embedded in the photo data. This can be a big problem if you post photos online (especially of kids) because it means that strangers might be able to extract the photo location. You can control whether the Camera app uses your location by launching the Settings app, tapping Privacy, tapping Location Services, tapping Camera, and then tapping Never or While Using the App.

Taking a photo

With the Camera app on-screen, here are the steps to run through to take a no-frills photo:

1. **Use the Mode switch (pointed out in Figure 6.4) to select Photo.**

2. **For a selfie, tap Switch Camera (again, see Figure 6.4) to use the front camera.**

3. **Compose your shot and then take the photo using one of the following techniques:**

- Tap the Camera app's Shutter button (pointed out in Figure 6.4).

- Press the iPad's Volume Up button.

4. **To view your photo, tap the Camera Roll button, which appears next to the Shutter button (see Figure 6.4).**

Learning the Camera app's features

Using the camera to take a basic shot is straightforward, but as you see in the rest of the chapter, Camera offers lots of ways to go beyond the basics. Before getting to those extra features, though, take a second to go over the Camera app features pointed out in Figure 6.4. I discuss these features in more detail in the sections that follow.

Zoom slider

Live Photos

Time Delay

Switch Camera

Shutter

Camera Roll

Mode switch

6.4 The features of the Camera app.

Focusing your shot

The Camera app offers an AutoFocus feature that automatically sets the focus on what's in the middle of the frame. What's that? Your subject isn't in the middle of the shot? No problem: Just tap the subject. The Camera app moves the focus to that object — and it shows the new focus location by displaying a square like the one pointed out in Figure 6.5. — and automatically adjusts the white balance and exposure.

Caution After you tap to set the focus, try to keep the tablet steady until you take the shot. If you move the iPad too much, AutoFocus will engage and change the focus to whatever is now in the center of the shot.

Focus rectangle

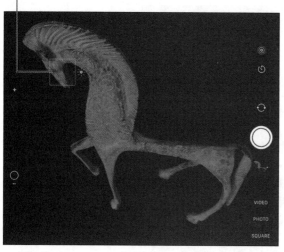

6.5 Tap the screen to set that location as the focus of the photo.

Locking the exposure and focus

Tapping the screen to set a custom focus point is a great feature. The problem is that once you have the perfect photo lined up and focused, it's *really* hard to keep the iPad steady enough to prevent AutoFocus from kicking in and wrecking the focus or exposure (or both!).

Fortunately, there is a solution called AutoExposure/AutoFocus Lock — AE/AF Lock, for short — which locks in your current exposure and focus no matter how much you move your iPad. It's a sweet feature, and you can give it a whirl by composing your shot and then long pressing the subject you want to focus on. When the focus rectangle pulses, release your finger. You now see AE/AF Lock at the top of the Camera app screen, as shown in Figure 6.6. This tells you that the current exposure and focus are locked, so you may fire when ready.

6.6 Long press the photo subject to lock the exposure and focus.

Zooming in and out of the shot

Your iPad's rear camera enables you to magnify — or *zoom* in on or out from — the subject of your shot. How you do this depends on your iPad:

- **iPad Pro 11-inch (2nd generation) and iPad Pro 12.9-inch (4th generation).** Tap the 1x icon to zoom out to 0.5x; tap 0.5x to zoom back in to 1x. Alternatively, long press the 1x icon and then drag the Zoom dial that appears to choose a magnification level between 0.5x and 5x.

- **All other models.** To zoom in, drag the Zoom slider (pointed out earlier in Figure 6.4) up; to zoom out, drag the Zoom slider down.

● **All models.** Spread two fingers on the screen to zoom out; pinch two fingers on the screen to zoom in.

Shooting live photos

When you take a shot, your iPad doesn't just record a single frame. Instead, the Camera app sneakily shoots a series of frames for 1.5 seconds before and 1.5 seconds after you tap the Shutter button. (Wait a minute, I hear you ask: How can the Camera app possibly shoot frames *before* I take my photo? Is it psychic? Nope: The Camera app is basically *always* recording those "before" frames; it just discards them if you don't take a shot.) The result? An animated photo that, when pressed and held in the Photos app, "plays" these frames, and you see what looks like a three-second video clip.

The Live Photos feature is automatically enabled on most iPads. If you don't like it, for whatever reason, you can turn it off by tapping the Live Photos icon (pointed out earlier in Figure 6.4).

Genius

If you're shooting some fast action, a single photo might not capture what you want. Instead, you can capture a burst of photos by pressing and holding the Shutter button. You can capture up to ten photos this way. To choose which photo you want to keep, tap Camera Roll, tap Select, tap the photo you want to preserve, tap Done, and then tap Keep Only 1 Favorite.

Shooting a panoramic photo

Your iPad lacks a wide-angle lens, but that doesn't mean you're out of luck when it comes to shooting extremely wide shots, especially landscapes. The Camera app offers a tool called Panorama that enables you to capture a scene by panning the iPad horizontally up to 240 degrees. Panorama takes advantage of the iPad's built-in gyroscope to align these images, even if your pan isn't perfectly level, and the result is a seamless, wide-angle image.

Here are the steps to follow to shoot a panoramic photo using the Camera app:

1. **Use the Mode switch to select Pano.** Camera switches to the Panorama tool, as shown in Figure 6.7.

2. **Point the camera at the leftmost part of the scene you want to shoot.** Yep, you can pan from right to left, if you prefer: Tap the arrow to switch direction.

3. **Tap Shutter to begin the shot.**

6.7 Set the Mode switch to Pano to display the Panorama tool.

4. **Pan the camera, keeping the following in mind:**

   ● Pan the camera steadily and continuously.

   ● Pan slowly. If Camera displays the message "Slow down," then you're panning too fast.

   ● Keep panning in the same direction. If you pan in the opposite direction, Camera ends the shot.

   ● Keep the arrow on the horizontal line as best you can.

   ● If the arrow moves under the line, tilt the top of the tablet toward you.

   ● If the arrow moves above the line, tilt the top of the tablet away from you.

5. **When your pan is done, tap Shutter.** Camera also ends the shot automatically when you've panned the full 240 degrees.

109

Shooting a photo with a time delay

Taking selfies with the iPad's front camera is easy enough, but it means holding a relatively heavy device at arm's length, which can all too often produce blurry self-portraits. The solution? Lean your iPad against a nearby vertical object or surface and then take advantage of Camera's time-delay tool, which tells Camera to wait for a specified number of seconds after you tap Shutter to shoot the photo. Here's how it works:

1. **Use Switch Camera to change to the iPad's front camera.**

2. **Lean the iPad against a vertical surface in a way that enables you to get into the frame when you're ready.**

3. **Tap Time Delay (pointed out earlier in Figure 6.4) and then tap the delay time interval you want to use: 3 seconds or 10 seconds.**

4. **Tap Shutter.**

5. **Place yourself into the shot before the time delay runs out.**

Reducing blurry iPad photos

The iPad camera hardware is gradually getting better, and the iPad generally takes really nice shots. However, probably the biggest problem most people have with iPad photos is blurry images, which are caused by not holding the tablet steady while taking the shot.

The latest iPads offer optical image stabilization, but still there are a few other things you can do to minimize or ideally eliminate blurred shots:

- Widen your stance to stabilize your body.

- Lean your shoulder (at least) or your entire side (at best) against any nearby object, such as a wall, doorframe, or car.

- Place your free arm across your torso with your forearm parallel to the ground; then rest the elbow of your "shooting" arm (that is, the one holding the iPad) on the free arm, which should help steady your shooting arm.

- Hold your breath while taking the shot.

- Remember that your iPad takes the shot when you *release* the Shutter button, not when you *press* it. Therefore, keep your subject composed and yourself steadied as best you can until you lift your finger off the Shutter button.

- After you release the Shutter button, keep the tablet steady until the photo thumbnail appears in the lower-left corner of the screen. If you move while the iPad is finalizing the photo, you'll blur the shot.

Keep some or all of these pointers in mind while shooting with your iPad, and you'll soon find that blurry iPad photos are a thing of the past.

How Can I Create Video on My iPad?

Your iPad's big screen makes it an ideal playback device for watching movies, TV shows, and other video content available via apps such as iTunes Store, Apple TV, and YouTube, not to mention that vast video library otherwise known as the web. But the iPad's copious screen real estate also means that it's an ideal device for editing recorded video, creating social media–friendly videos with the Clips app, and making your own cinematic masterpieces with the iMovie app. Whether you have ambitions to be the next Steven Spielberg or Greta Gerwig or you just want to make your Instagram friends smile, your iPad is the ideal outlet for your video creativity.

Recording Video

The latest iPads are a bit lighter and quite a bit thinner than the original iPad, but they're still a bit too big and heavy for regular use as a digital video camera. The iPad mini is smaller (it's about half the weight of the iPad), but it's still a slightly odd choice to use as a camcorder. You probably won't find yourself using your tablet to record video all that often. On the other hand, the iPad cameras aren't too shabby when it comes to video:

● **Rear camera.** For the iPad Pro and the iPad Air, this camera supports 4K (3840×2160) video recording at 24, 30, or 60 frames per second (fps), whereas the iPad and iPad mini rear camera supports recording 1080p HD recording at 30 fps.

● **Front camera.** For the iPad Pro, iPad Air, and iPad mini, this camera supports 1080p HD video recording, whereas the iPad's front camera supports 720p HD recording.

All iPads also offer video stabilization, which reduces the effects of camera shake, and a Slo-Mo video mode that captures either 1080p video at 120 or 240 fps (on the iPad Pro) or 720p video at 120 fps (on all other iPad models).

These are impressive numbers, so if a must-record event suddenly arises and you don't have your digital camera (or iPhone) with you, then shooting video with your iPad will certainly do in a pinch.

Note

You might be wondering what that *p* stands for in video formats such as 1080p and 720p. It's short for *progressive scanning*, and it means that each horizontal line in a video frame gets drawn on the screen in sequence (first line, then second line, and so on). This is in contrast to *interlaced scanning*, which first draws the odd-numbered lines and then draws the even-numbered lines. Interlaced scanning creates an annoying flickering effect, so progressive is the better technology.

Recording video on your iPad

Here are the basic steps to follow to shoot a video (regular or slow motion) using your iPad:

1. **Launch the Camera app using one of the following methods:**

   ● On the Home screen, tap the Camera app.

   ● Display the Control Center and then tap the Camera icon.

   ● From the Lock screen, swipe left.

2. **Slide the Mode switch to Video.** Figure 7.1 shows the Camera app in Video mode. If you want to shoot in slow motion, slide the Mode switch to Slo-Mo instead.

Zoom slider   Video duration

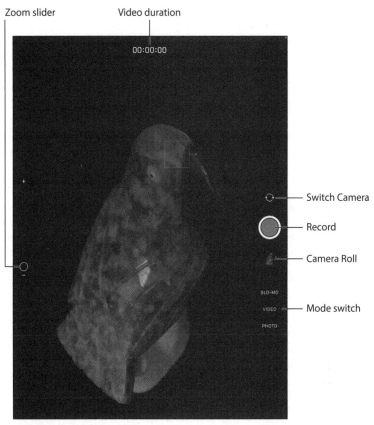

Switch Camera

Record

Camera Roll

Mode switch

7.1 The Camera app in Video mode.

3. **Use the Switch Camera button to select which of the iPad's cameras you want to use.**

4. **If you're using the rear camera, use the Zoom slider to set the video magnification.**

5. **Tap the red Record button.** The Camera app starts the video recording. The total recording time appears at the top of the screen.

6. **When you're finished, tap the Record button once again to stop the recording.** The Camera app saves the video to your iPad's Camera Roll.

115

Genius

To easily locate your recorded videos, open the Photos app, tap Back (<) until you see the Photos pane, and then tap Videos in the Media Types section. Depending on the Video mode you used, you can alternatively tap Slo-Mo or Time-Lapse (covered in the next section).

Shooting a time-lapse video

Some scenes change over time, and a popular photographic technique is to take a series of still images at regular intervals — for example, every 10 seconds or every minute. This is called *time-lapse* photography and doing this by hand is problematic for two reasons: You have to remember to do it, and you have to make sure the camera is positioned in the same spot for each photo.

Fortunately, the Camera app solves both problems by offering Time-Lapse mode, which shoots a video of a scene by automatically snapping a photo every six seconds and then combining these stills into a single video. (So, for example, recording in Time-Lapse mode for 60 seconds produces a 10-second video.) This saves you the hassle of taking individual shots as well as freeing up the storage space required for a full-blown video.

To shoot a time-lapse video, set the Camera app's Mode switch to Time-Lapse and then tap the Record button. A progress bar forms a circle around the Record button every six seconds, and each time that circle completes, Camera takes another still image.

Setting the recording format for video and slow motion

Video recording tends to eat storage space at an alarming rate. If you shoot a lot of video and your iPad's storage is getting low, consider changing the video format as follows:

- Drop the resolution from 1080p to 720p.
- Drop the frames per second from 60 fps to 30 fps or 24 fps.

Depending on your iPad model, you can make these changes both for regular video recording and for slow-motion recording. Here are the steps to follow:

1. **Open the Settings app.**

2. **Tap Camera.** The Camera settings appear.

3. **To change the video format, tap Record Video and then tap the format you want to use, such as 720p HD at 30 fps.** Tap Back (<) to return to the Camera settings.

Genius

If you want to be able to switch the video format from within the Camera app, tap the Video Format Control switch to On. Restart the Camera app, select the Video mode, and you see a new Video Format control to the right of the time at the top of the screen. Tap the control to cycle through the available video formats.

4. **(iPad Pro and iPad Air only) To change the slow-motion video format, tap Record Slo-mo and then tap the format you want to use, such as 1080p HD at 120 fps.**

Editing Recorded Video

When you record video on your iPad, the biggest problem you run into is extraneous footage that appears at the beginning or the end of the clip (usually both). Not to worry, though: Your iPad has your back by enabling you to cut — or *trim*, in the video vernacular — unneeded scenes from the beginning and end of the file. Here are the steps to follow to trim a video right on your tablet:

1. **Open the Photos app.**

2. **Tap Back (<) until you see the Photos pane and then tap Videos in the Media Types section.**

3. **Tap the video you want to edit.** The Photos app displays the video and a Timeline of the video along the top of the screen.

Note

If you're working in a Photos app library that includes both photos and videos, you can differentiate between these by noting that video thumbnails show the duration of the video in the lower right corner.

4. **Drag the left edge of the Timeline to specify the start of the footage you want to keep.** Everything to the left of this point will be discarded.

5. **Drag the right edge of the Timeline to specify the end of the footage you want to keep.** Everything to the right of this point will be discarded. Figure 7.2 shows an example of a video ready to be trimmed.

117

Start of the footage to keep   End of the footage to keep

7.2 To trim a video, use the Timeline to specify the starting and ending points of the video footage you want to keep.

6. **Tap Play to check that you've set the trim points correctly.** Photos plays just the video between the trim points. If things don't look right, repeat Steps 3 and 4 to adjust the trim points as needed.

7. **Tap Done.** Photos trims the video.

Creating Videos with the Clips App

Videos recorded with the Camera app certainly get the job done, but in this social media–obsessed age, those videos lack a certain panache that might make you think twice about sharing them. Sure, as I discuss later in this chapter, the iMovie app gives you tons of video bells and whistles to play around with, but iMovie's sophisticated features are probably overkill if all you want to do is post a short clip for your friends and followers.

A better way to go is to use the Clips app to create the video you want to share. You can add filters, live captions, still images, and more, and then easily share the resulting video. The next few sections provide the details.

Creating a Clips video

Launch the Clips app from the iPad Home screen, and you immediately end up in the recording screen, shown in Figure 7.3. (If you're starting Clips for the first time, the app takes you through a short introduction first.)

7.3 The recording mode of the Clips app.

Here are the steps to follow to create a video using the Clips app:

1. **To apply an effect to your clip, tap the Effects icon.** The dialog that appears offers five types of effect:

   - **Filters.** Applies a special effect to the video, such as the Comic Book effect shown in Figure 7.4.

   - **Live Titles.** Overlays various styles of text that you speak aloud during the recording.

   - **Text.** Overlays preset (but editable, if needed) text in a variety of styles. After you add the text, you can drag it to your preferred location.

Play   Live Titles   Stickers   Emoji

Filters   Text

7.4 You can apply filters and other effects to your video.

- **Stickers.** Overlays an emoji sticker, such as a heart or flames. After you add the sticker, you can drag it to your preferred location.

- **Emoji.** Overlays an emoji. After you add the emoji, you can drag it to your preferred location.

2. **Create a new clip using one of the following techniques:**

- **Create a video clip.** To create a video clip, first use the Switch Camera button to select which iPad camera you want to use and then press and hold the Record button. Clips begins recording your video. When your video clip is complete, release the Record button. Clips adds a thumbnail for the video clip to the Timeline at the bottom of the screen.

Genius

If you need both hands free during the recording, notice the little lock icon that appears to the left of the Record button while you're holding it down. Slide your finger over to the lock icon. Release your finger, and Clips will continue to record video. If you do this, then to stop the recording you need to tap the Record button again.

- **Create a clip by taking a photo.** To take a photo to use as a clip, line up your shot, tap the Shutter button, and then press and hold the Record button for the number of seconds that you want the photo to be displayed in your video. When you release Record, Clips adds a thumbnail for the photo clip to the Timeline.

- **Create a clip from an existing image.** To use an existing photo as a clip, tap the Photos button, tap the image you want to use, and then press and hold the Record button for the number of seconds that you want the image to be displayed. When you release Record, Clips adds a thumbnail for the image clip to the Timeline.

3. **Repeat Steps 1 and 2 to add all the clips you want to include in your video.**

4. **To rearrange the clips, long press a clip thumbnail and then drag it along the Timeline to the position you want.**

5. **To play music during your video, tap Music and then tap one of the following:**

- **Soundtracks.** Offers a selection of predefined background sounds.

- **My Music.** Enables you to choose a song from your music library.

6. **To set the aspect ratio for your video, tap Aspect and then tap the aspect ratio you want to use.**

121

7. **To preview your video, tap Play to the left of the Timeline.**

8. **To name your video, tap Projects, tap your video, tap More (the three dots in the upper right corner), tap Rename, type the new name, and then tap Save.** To return to your project, tap Done.

9. **To save your video to your Photos library, tap Share and then tap Save Video.**

Adding a new Clips project

Once you create one Clips video, you'll want to create another one right away. No problem! Here are the steps to follow to start a fresh project:

1. **Tap Projects.** Clips takes you to the Projects screen.

2. **Tap Create New (+).** Clips starts a new project for you.

Making Movies with iMovie

Earlier I show you the built-in editing feature that comes with the iPad, which essentially boils down to being able to trim video clips. That's pretty handy, but proper video editing requires features such as adding transitions and titles, changing the theme, and adding a music track. Fortunately, you can do all that and more using the powerful iMovie app. With iMovie, you can perform many of the same tasks that you can using the desktop iMovie application, such as importing live or recorded videos and photos, trimming clips, adding transitions, applying a Ken Burns effect to a photo, adding titles and music tracks, applying themes, and much more.

Creating a new iMovie project

To get started, tap the iMovie icon. In the opening screen, follow these steps to create a fresh iMovie project:

1. **Tap the Create Project (+) button.** iMovie asks if you want to create a movie or trailer.

2. **Tap Movie.** iMovie prompts you to add some content.

3. **Go ahead and select one or more videos or photos you want to use.** This is optional for now, and I show you how to add content in more detail later in this chapter (see "Importing media into your project").

4. **Tap Create Movie.** iMovie saves your new project and adds it to the Projects list.

Opening a project for editing

For the rest of this chapter, you'll be working within a specific project, so go ahead and select Back (<) until you get to the Projects screen, tap the project you want to work with, and then tap Edit. You end up in the iMovie project-editing environment. Figure 7.5 shows an example of the editing environment for a project that already has clips and other media imported.

7.5 You see a screen similar to this when you open a video for editing in iMovie.

There are three main elements in the iMovie editing environment:

- **Timeline.** This is the strip in the bottom half of the screen. It displays your video clips, photos, transitions, and audio track.

- **Playback window.** This is the larger pane that takes up most of the top half of the window. It shows your video when you play it and when you scroll through the Timeline.

- **Tools.** These appear throughout the playback window. There are eight tools (pointed out in Figure 7.5):

  - **Settings.** Sets various project options.

  - **Add Media.** Imports existing videos, photos, and music.

  - **Toggle Audio Waveforms.** Shows or hides the waveforms for the video's audio track.

  - **Undo.** Reverses your most recent action.

  - **Play.** Runs the movie.

  - **Rewind to Beginning.** Returns the video to the start.

  - **Camera.** Imports videos or photos shot with an iPad camera.

  - **Record Audio.** Records a voiceover track for the video.

Importing media into your project

With your new project on the go, your first task is to import media into it. With iMovie, you can import four kinds of media: recorded video, existing video, photos, and music (which I cover later in this chapter).

Importing a video from an iPad camera

You can record whatever is happening around you and import it directly into your iMovie project using one of the built-in iPad cameras. Here's how you do it:

1. **Open your iMovie project.**

2. **Scroll through the Timeline to the location where you want the video to appear.**

3. **Tap the Camera icon and then tap Allow if iMovie requests your current location.** Your iPad switches to the Camera app, which activates the Video mode switch.

4. **Tap the Switch Camera icon to choose a different camera, if necessary.**

5. **Tap the screen to focus the video, if necessary.**

6. **Tap the red Record button.** Your iPad starts recording video and displays the total recording time in the upper right corner of the screen.

7. **When you're done, tap the Record button again to stop recording.** iMovie displays a preview of the recorded video.

8. **If the video looks good, tap Use Video to add it to the Timeline.** Otherwise, tap Retake and then reshoot the video.

Importing existing video

If you've already recorded your video or synced one from your computer, you can add it to your project Timeline. Here are the steps to follow:

1. **Open your iMovie project.**

2. **Scroll through the Timeline to the location where you want the video to appear.**

3. **Tap the Add Media icon.** iMovie displays the importing screen.

4. **Tap Video.**

5. **Tap a category, such as All or Recently Added.** iMovie displays thumbnails of the videos in the category you selected.

6. **Scroll through the videos until you find the one you want to import.**

7. **Tap the video.** If you see the Download icon (meaning that the video is available in the cloud but not on your iPad), tap the Download icon.

8. **Tap Add (+).** iMovie adds it to the Timeline.

Importing a photo from the camera

You can take a still image and import it directly into your iMovie project using one of the built-in cameras on your iPad. Here's how you do it:

1. **Open your iMovie project.**

2. **Scroll through the Timeline to the location where you want the video to appear.**

3. **Tap the Camera icon.** Your iPad switches to the camera.

4. **Flick the Mode switch from Video to Photo.**

5. **Tap the screen to focus the photo, if necessary.**

6. **Tap the Shutter button.** Your iPad takes the photo and displays a preview of the result.

7. **If the photo looks good, tap Use Photo to add it to the Timeline.** Otherwise, tap Retake and then reshoot the photo.

Importing an existing photo

You can also import a photo to your project, which iMovie automatically animates by applying a five-second-long Ken Burns effect (which is a pan-and-zoom effect popularized by filmmaker Ken Burns). Follow these steps to add a photo to your project:

1. **Open your iMovie project.**

2. **Scroll through the Timeline to the location where you want the photo to appear.**

3. **Tap the Import icon.** iMovie displays the importing screen.

4. **Tap Photos.** iMovie displays the Photos screen.

5. **Tap the album that contains the photo you want to import.** iMovie displays thumbnails of the album's photos.

6. **Tap the photo.** If you see the Download icon (meaning that the photo is available in the cloud but not on your iPad), tap the Download icon.

7. **Tap Add (+).** iMovie adds the photo to the Timeline.

Working with video clips

iMovie gives you a surprisingly complete collection of video-editing tools that enable you to move and trim clips, change transitions, work with a photo's Ken Burns effect, and add clip titles.

Moving a clip

If a clip doesn't appear where you want it, follow these steps to move it to the position you prefer:

1. **Tap and hold the middle of the clip you want to move.**

2. **Drag the clip left or right through the Timeline.**

3. **Drop the clip when you reach the location you want.** iMovie moves the clip.

Trimming a clip

If an imported video clip includes footage at the beginning or end (or both) that you don't want to include in your movie, you can trim those unwanted scenes. Here are the steps to follow:

1. **Tap the clip you want to trim.** iMovie displays the trim controls, as shown in Figure 7.6.

Left trim control   Right trim control

7.6 Tap a clip to display the trimming tools.

Genius

For more precise trimming, spread your fingers on the clip to expand it in the Timeline. If you go too far, pinch the clip to shrink it.

2. **Drag the left trim control to set the starting point of the clip.**

3. **Drag the right trim control to set the ending point of the clip.**

4. **Tap the playback window.** iMovie saves your changes.

Changing the transition between two clips

iMovie makes transitions a no-brainer because it adds them automatically between any two clips when you add videos or photos to the Timeline. It also defines different transitions for each theme applied to a project. (I show you how to change themes a bit later.) If you don't like the theme transitions, you can switch to one of the built-in transitions (such as Dissolve, where the end of one clip dissolves into the beginning of the next), or you can turn off the transition altogether. You can also vary the length of the transition.

Here are the steps to follow:

1. **Tap the transition you want to change.** iMovie displays the Transition Settings window, shown in Figure 7.7.

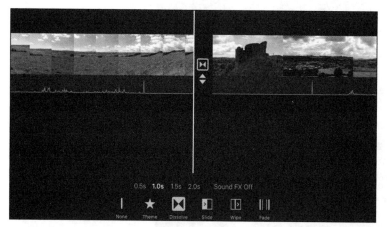

7.7 Tap the transition to open the Transition Settings window.

2. **Tap the transition you want: Theme, a built-in effect (Dissolve, Slide, Wipe, or Fade), or None.**

3. **Tap the length of the transition in seconds: 0.5s, 1.0s, or 1.5s.**

4. **Tap the playback window.** iMovie saves the transition settings.

Adjusting a photo's Ken Burns effect

I mention earlier that when you import a photo, iMovie automatically applies a Ken Burns effect, which pans and zooms the photo. You can control the panning and zooming by following these steps:

1. **Tap the photo you want to edit.** iMovie selects the photo and displays the Ken Burns effect tools, as shown in Figure 7.8.

7.8 Tap the photo to display the Ken Burns effect tools.

2. **Tap Start.**

3. **Set the opening zoom level by pinching or spreading on the photo.**

4. **Set the starting position of the pan by using the playback window to drag the photo to the position you prefer.**

5. **Tap End.**

6. **Set the closing zoom level by pinching or spreading on the photo.**

7. **Set the ending position of the pan by using the playback window to drag the photo to the position you prefer.**

8. **Tap Start and then tap Play to check the effect is what you want.** If you need to make changes, repeat Steps 2 through 7.

Adding a title to a clip

You can get your movie off to a proper start by adding a title to your opening clip. iMovie offers a number of title styles that you can choose from, and it offers quite a few options for getting the title to look the way you want. Follow these steps to add a title to any clip:

1. **Tap the clip you want to work with.** iMovie displays the clip tools.

2. **Tap Titles.** iMovie displays the title tools.

3. **Tap the title style you want.**

4. **Tap the Title Text Here text box, tap Edit, type the title you want to use, and then tap outside the text box.**

5. **Drag the title to the position you prefer.**

6. **Set the title size by pinching or spreading on the title text.**

7. **Set the title font (the Aa icon), color (the circle icon), and options (the three dots icon).**

8. **Tap the playback screen.** iMovie adds the title to the clip.

Genius

By default, the title appears on-screen for four seconds. If you'd prefer to have the title appear for the full length of the clip, tap Options (the three dots) and then tap the Full Clip Duration switch to On.

Removing a clip

If you add a clip accidentally or decide a clip is no longer needed, you can use either of the following techniques to remove it from your project:

● Tap the clip to display the clip menu bar and then tap Delete.

● Long press the clip and then drag the clip up and off the Timeline. When you release the clip, iMovie deletes it.

Working with your project

Your iMovie project is coming along nicely, with its trimmed clips, transitions, Ken Burns effects, and titles. What else can iMovie do? Four things, actually: add music, change the theme, give your project a cool name, and export your project to a movie file.

Adding a music track

What would a video be without a music track playing in the background? Boring, that's what! Fortunately, iMovie lets you add either a song from your Music library or an audio track from the project's current theme. Here's how it works:

1. **Tap the Add Media icon.** iMovie displays the Import screen.

2. **Tap Back (<) until you get to the Media pane.**

3. **Tap the Audio tab at the bottom of the Media pane.** iMovie displays the Audio pane.

4. **Tap the music category you want to use.** To use an audio track from the project's theme, tap Soundtracks; to insert a sound effect, tap Sound Effects; otherwise, tap My Music and then tap a category, such as Playlists, Albums, or Artists.

5. **Locate the track you want to add.** For example, if you selected the Artists category, you'd need to select an artist and then an album.

6. **Tap the track and then tap Add (+).** iMovie adds the track to the bottom of the Timeline, as shown in Figure 7.9.

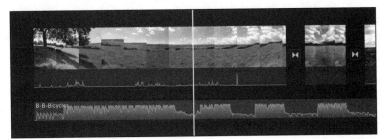

7.9 After you select a song or audio track, iMovie displays the track as a green strip at the bottom of the Timeline.

Changing the project theme

The secret to easy iMovie-making is the project theme. As you've seen, the project theme enables you to automatically apply clip transitions, title styles, and music tracks to give your movie a cohesive and consistent feel. iMovie ships with five built-in themes, so you can pick the one that best complements your movie subject. Follow these steps to change the project theme:

1. **Open your iMovie project.**

2. **Tap the Settings icon.** iMovie displays the Project Settings screen, as shown in Figure 7.10.

3. **Tap the theme you want to use.**

4. **If you want to apply a filter to the project, tap an item in the Project Filter section.**

5. **If you want to use the music tracks that come with the theme, tap the Theme Soundtrack switch to On.**

6. **To control how the movie fades in and out, tap either or both of the Fade In From Black and Fade Out to Black switches to On.**

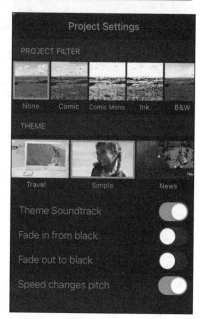

7.10 In the Project Settings screen, tap a theme.

7. **Tap Done.** iMovie saves your settings and updates the project with the new theme.

Naming your project

Your movie just isn't complete without a snappy title, so follow these steps to name your project:

1. **If you have your project open in the editing environment, tap Done to return to the project's main screen.**

2. **Tap the project's existing title.** iMovie opens the title for editing.

3. **Type the movie title.**

4. **Tap Done.**

Exporting your project

With your clips imported and trimmed, your transitions and titles in place, your music added and your theme applied, your movie is finally ready for prime time. Although you can play the movie within the editing environment (by tapping the Play button), you won't really be able to show it off until you export it to a movie file. iMovie gives you four choices: HD - 1080p, HD - 720p, Large - 540p, or Medium - 360p.

Follow these steps to export your project to your iPad's photo library:

1. **If you have your project open in the editing environment, tap Done to return to the project's main screen.**

2. **Tap the Share icon.** iMovie displays a list of actions you can perform.

3. **Tap Save Video.** iMovie exports the project to a movie file, which it then stores in the Videos album within the Photos app.

How Do I Manage My Contacts?

Before the Internet came along, people used an "address book" to keep track of the people they knew, which usually consisted of written entries containing just two things for each person: a home phone number and a home address. Now, well into the third decade of the twenty-first century, it's hard to imagine having just two bits of contact info for the people in your life. These days, most folks have not only a phone number (a cell number, not a landline number) and a physical address, but also one or more social media handles, a website address, and on and on. So, an "address book" is more important than ever, but nowadays the modern version is electronic and, on the iPad, it comes in the form of the Contacts app, which is chock full of features that can help you keep track of all the people in your life.

Getting Started with Contacts

You need Contacts up and running for this chapter, so head for the Home screen and tap the Contacts icon. Contacts is best used in landscape mode, which shows the Contacts pane on the left and the currently selected contact on the right, as shown in Figure 8.1. (If you prefer to work in portrait mode, you can display the Contacts pane by tapping the Back (<) button.)

8.1 In landscape mode, you see the Contacts pane on the left and the current contact's details on the right.

If you have a healthy number of contacts, you need to know how to navigate the Contacts list. You have the following three choices:

- **Flick up and down to scroll through the list.**

- **Tap a letter on the right side of the Contacts pane to leap directly to the contacts whose last names begin with that letter.**

- Use the Search box at the top of the Contacts list to type a few letters of the name of the contact you want to view and then tap the contact in the search results.

Creating a Contact

The next time you realize someone's missing from your contacts, you can fire up your trusty tablet and follow these steps to tap that person's vital statistics right into the Contacts app:

1. **Open the Contacts app.**

2. **In the top right corner of the Contacts pane, tap New Contact (+).** Contacts displays the New Contact dialog, as shown in Figure 8.2.

8.2 Use the New Contact dialog to enter your new contact's details.

3. **Use the First Name field to type the contact's given name.** If you're entering the contact data for a company or other organization, skip ahead to Step 5.

4. **Use the Last Name field to type the contact's surname.**

5. **Use the Company field to type either the contact's place of business or the name of the business you're adding as a contact.**

Yup, I know there are still plenty of other fields to fill in, and we get to those in a second. For now, though, I want to interrupt your regularly scheduled programming to show you how to edit an existing contact. It will all make sense soon, trust me.

Genius

If you have a Mac, remember that you can start creating or editing a contact on your iPad and then use the Handoff feature to continue working with that contact on your Mac. When your iPad comes within range of your Mac, click the Contacts icon that appears to the left of the macOS Dock.

Editing a Contact

Now that your new contact is off to a flying start, you can go ahead and fill in details, such as phone numbers, addresses (email, web, and snail mail), and anything else you want to add (or have the patience to enter into the New Contact screen). The next few sections take you through the steps for each type of data.

However, the techniques I present also apply if you want to edit any contact that's already residing in your iPad's Contacts app. Here are the general steps to follow to edit an existing contact:

1. **Tap the contact you want to edit.**

2. **Tap Edit.** Contacts opens the contact's data for editing.

3. **Make your edits, as I describe in the next few sections.**

4. **Tap Done.** Contacts saves your edits and takes the contact out of editing mode.

Assigning phone numbers to a contact

Everyone has a phone number, so it makes sense to begin by entering that person's phone data. Sure, but which number: Work? Home? Mobile? School? Fortunately, there's no need to choose just one because Contacts is happy to store all of these, plus a few more if needed.

Follow these steps to add one or more phone numbers for a contact:

1. **With the contact's data open for editing, tap Add Phone.** Contacts creates a new phone field.

2. **Type the phone number with area code first.** Note that you only need to type the numbers — Contacts helpfully adds extra stuff, like parentheses around the area code and the dash.

3. **Examine the label box in the Phone field to see if the default label (it's usually** *mobile*) **is the one you want.** If you're okay with the existing label, skip to Step 5; otherwise, tap the label to open the Label dialog, shown in Figure 8.3.

Cancel	Label	Edit
mobile		✓
home		
work		
school		
iPhone		
main		
home fax		
work fax		
pager		
other		
Add Custom Label		

8.3 Tap the label you want to use for a contact's phone number.

4. **Tap the label that best applies to the phone number you're adding, such as mobile, home, or work.** Contacts displays the new label.

5. **Repeat Steps 1 to 4 to add any other numbers you want to store for this contact.** Note that each time you add a number, Contacts creates a new Add Phone field below the current field, and you tap that field to add a new number.

Assigning email addresses to a contact

It makes sense that you might want to add multiple phone numbers for a contact, but would you ever need to enter multiple email addresses? Well, sure you would! Most people have at least a couple of addresses — usually a personal address and a work address — and some Type-A emailers have a dozen or more. Life is too short to type that many email addresses, but you do need at least the important ones if you want to use the Mail app to send a message to a contact.

Follow these steps to add one or more email addresses for a contact:

1. **With the contact's data open for editing, tap Add Email.** Contacts creates a new email field.

2. **Type the person's email address.**

3. **Tap the label beside the new Email field and then use the Label dialog to tap the label that best applies to the email address you're adding, such as home, work, or school.** Contacts displays the new label.

4. **Feel free to repeat Steps 1 to 3 to add more email addresses for this contact.**

Assigning web addresses to a contact

Who on Earth doesn't have a website these days? It could be a humble home page, a blog, or a home business site, or it could be someone's corporate website. Whatever web home a person has, it's a good idea to toss the address into her contact data because, later, you can tap the address, and Contacts (assuming your tablet can see the Internet from here) immediately fires up Safari, which takes you to the site.

You can add a web address for a contact by making your way through these steps:

1. **Open the contact's data for editing.**

2. **Tap Add URL.** Contacts creates a new URL field and displays the keyboard, as shown in Figure 8.4. Note, in particular, the colon (:), slash (/), underscore (_), dash (-), and .com keys along the bottom row of the on-screen keyboard, which come in handy when entering a web address.

3. **Type the person's web address.**

4. **Tap the label beside the new URL field and then use the Label dialog to tap the label that best applies to the web address you're adding, such as homepage or work.** Contacts displays the new label.

8.4 Don't forget to take advantage of the on-screen keyboard's URL-friendly keys, such as slash (/) and .com.

Genius

To save some wear and tear on your tapping finger, don't bother adding the http:// stuff at the beginning of a URL. Safari adds those characters automatically whenever you tap an address to visit a site — same with the www. prefix. So if the full address is http://www.mcfedries.com/, you need only enter mcfedries.com.

Assigning social media data to a contact

These days, many of us are far more likely to contact others via social media (such as Twitter, Facebook, and LinkedIn) than we are via more traditional methods like email. Contacts reflects this new reality by enabling you to save social media data for each contact, including data for Twitter, Facebook, LinkedIn, Flickr, and Skype. Here are the steps to follow to add one or more social media details to a contact:

1. **With the contact's data open for editing, tap Add Social Profile.** Contacts creates a new Social Profile field.

2. **Type the username or handle the person uses for the selected social media.**

3. **To specify a different social media service, tap the Twitter label to see a list of social media platforms, as shown in Figure 8.5, and then tap the label that suits the social media data you're entering, such as Facebook or Flickr.** Contacts adds the new label.

4. **If necessary, repeat Steps 1 to 3 to add other social media details, as needed.**

141

Genius

If you don't see the social media platform that your contact uses (TikTok? Instagram? WhatsApp?), tap Add Custom Service and then type the name of the platform in the text box that appears.

Cancel	
Skype	
Twitter	✓
Facebook	
Flickr	
LinkedIn	
Myspace	
Sina Weibo	
Add Custom Service	

8.5 Tap Twitter to see the social networks supported by Contacts.

Assigning physical addresses to a contact

With all this talk about cell numbers, email and web addresses, and social networks, it's easy to forget that people actually live and work somewhere. You may have plenty of contacts where the location of that somewhere doesn't much matter, but if you ever need to get from here to there, taking the time to insert a contact's physical address really pays off. Why? Because you need only tap the address and Contacts switches to Maps to show you the precise location. From there you can get directions, see a satellite map of the area, and more. (I talk about all this great map stuff in Chapter 10.)

Tapping out a full address is a bit of work, but as the following steps show, it's not exactly painful:

1. **With the contact's data open for editing, tap Add Address.** Contacts displays the address fields.

2. **Tap the first Street field and then type the person's street address.**

3. **(Optional) Tap the second Street field and then type even more of the person's street address.**

4. **Tap the City field and then type the person's city.**

5. **Tap the State field and then type the person's state.** Depending on what you later select for the country, this field might have a different name, such as Province.

6. **Tap the ZIP field and then type the ZIP code.** Again, depending on what you later select for the country, this field might have a different name, such as Postal Code.

7. **Tap the Country field to open the Country list and then tap the contact's country.**

8. **Examine the label box to see if the default label is the one you want.** If it is, skip to Step 10; if it's not, tap the label box to open the Label screen.

9. **Tap the label that best applies to the physical address you're inserting (Contacts automatically sends you back to the contact's data screen after you tap), such as home or work.**

10. **Repeat Steps 1 to 9 if you feel like entering another address for your contact.**

Adding a photo to a contact

For each new contact, Contacts assigns a default "photo" that consists of the person's first and last initials. Boring! To jazz things up a bit, you can replace those initials with an existing photo, a new photo, an emoji, or custom text. Here's what you do:

1. **Open the contact for editing.**

2. **Tap Add Photo.** Contacts displays its tools for adding a photo, as shown in Figure 8.6.

3. **Tap one of the following icons to select an image for the contact:**

   ● **Camera.** Opens the Camera app so that you can take a photo of the contact. Move and scale the resulting photo as needed and then tap Use Photo.

   ● **Photos.** Displays the Photos window. Locate and tap the photo you want to assign, move and scale the photo as needed, and then tap Choose.

   ● **Emoji.** Displays a blank circle. Tap an Emoji to place it inside the circle, use the Style tab to select a style, and then tap Done.

   ● **Edit.** Opens the default photo (the contact's initials) for editing. Type the one or two characters you prefer to use and then tap Done.

   ● **Memoji.** Tap a character in the Memoji section, move and scale the image as needed, and then tap Choose.

4. **Tap Done.** Contacts adds the photo to the contact.

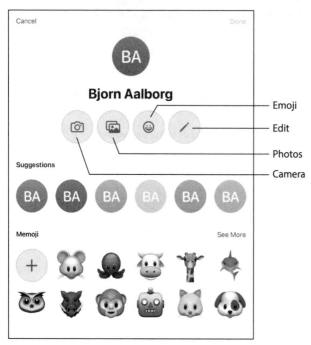

8.6 Use this dialog to add a photo or other image to a contact.

Deleting a contact

It feels good to add new contacts, but you don't get a lifetime guarantee with these things: Friends fall out or fade away, colleagues decide to make a new start at another firm, clients take their business elsewhere, and some of your acquaintances simply wear out their welcome after a while. You move on and so does your Contacts list. The best way to proceed is to delete the contact and keep the list trim and tidy.

Follow these steps to delete a contact:

1. **Tap the contact you want to delete.**

2. **Tap Edit.** The contact's data screen appears.

3. **Tap the Delete Contact button at the bottom of the screen.** Contacts asks you to confirm the deletion.

4. **Tap Delete Contact.** Contacts removes the contact.

Getting More Out of Contacts

Adding and editing data using Contacts is blissfully linear: Tap a field label to change it and then tap inside a field to add the data. If you remember to take advantage of the on-screen keyboard context-sensitive keys (such as the .com key that materializes when you type a web address), then contact data entry becomes a snap.

Contacts is straightforward on the surface, but if you dig a bit deeper, you find some useful tools and features that can make your contact management duties even easier.

Creating a custom field label

When you add information to a contact, you add not only the data itself, but also a label that describes the data. Common labels are *home*, *work*, *school*, and *mobile*. These are most useful when you have multiple instances of contact data such as phone numbers and email addresses because the labels make it easier to differentiate between them.

If the preset labels don't fit a particular tidbit of contact data, one solution would be to select the *other* label. However, that's not very descriptive (to say the least!), so you're almost always better off taking a few extra seconds to create a custom label, like so:

1. **Tap the contact you want to work with.**

2. **Tap Edit.** The contact's data opens for editing.

3. **Tap the label beside the field for which you want to create the custom label.** The Label dialog appears.

4. **Tap Add Custom Label.** Contacts adds a new blank line to the Label dialog.

5. **Type your custom label.**

6. **Tap Done.** Contacts saves your custom label and applies it to the contact field.

Contacts remembers your custom label, which means you're free to apply it to any type of contact data. For example, you can create a label named *university* and apply it to a phone number, an email address, a web address, or a physical address.

Adding fields to a contact

The New Contact screen (which appears when you add a contact) and the editing screen (which appears when you edit an existing contact) display only the fields you need for

145

basic contact info. In addition to the fields I've covered so far, you can click the following items to add more fields to a contact's data:

- **Add Birthday.** Tap this item to add the contact's day, month, and year of birth.

- **Add Date.** Tap this item to add any other date, such as an anniversary.

- **Add Related Name.** Tap this item to specify another contact who is related to the contact you're editing. For example, if you also have the contact's brother in your Contacts list, tap Add Related Name, tap More Info (the *i* icon), tap the brother, tap the field label (the default is *mother*), and then tap the relationship type.

- **Add Instant Message.** Tap this item to add the contact's instant messaging data for a service such as Skype, Google Talk, or AIM.

- **Notes.** Use this field to add general observations or contact data that doesn't fit into any other field.

Despite these additional fields, the contact data screen still lacks quite a few common fields. For example, you might need to specify a contact's prefix (such as Dr. or Professor), suffix (such as Jr., Sr., or III), or job title.

Thankfully, Contacts is merely hiding these and other useful fields where you can't see them. There are 13 hidden fields that you can add to any contact, as shown in Figure 8.7. Contacts is only too happy to let you add as many of these extra fields as you want. Follow these steps to do so:

1. **With the contact's data open for editing, tap Add Field.** The Add Field dialog appears, as shown in Figure 8.7.

2. **Tap the field that you want to add.** Contacts adds the field to the contact.

3. **If the field has a label, tap the label box to choose a new one if needed.**

4. **Type the field data.** In the case of the Related Name field, tap the label (the default value is *mother*), tap the relationship (such as spouse or manager), tap the More Info (*i*) icon, and then tap the related contact.

5. **Repeat Steps 1 to 4 to add more fields as needed.**

Deleting fields from a contact

People change, and so does their contact info. Most of the time these changes require you to edit an existing field, but sometimes people actually shed information. For example, they might get rid of a pager or fax machine, or they might shutter a website. Whatever the reason, you should delete that data from the contact to keep the data screen tidy and easier to navigate.

Cancel	Add Field
Prefix	
Phonetic first name	
Pronunciation first name	
Middle name	
Phonetic middle name	
Phonetic last name	
Pronunciation last name	
Maiden name	
Suffix	
Nickname	
Job title	
Department	
Phonetic company name	

8.7 The Add Field dialog shows the hidden fields that you can add to any contact.

To delete a contact field, follow these steps:

1. **In the Contacts list, tap the contact with which you want to work.**

2. **Tap Edit.** The editing screen appears.

3. **Tap the red Delete button to the left of the field you want to trash.** Contacts displays a Delete button to the right of the field.

4. **Tap Delete.** Contacts removes the field.

5. **Tap Done.** Contacts closes the editing screen.

Creating a new contact from a vCard

Typing a person's contact data is a tedious bit of business at the best of times, so it helps if you can find a faster way to do it. If you can cajole a contact into sending his or her contact data electronically, then you can add that data with just a couple of taps.

147

What do I mean when I talk about sending contact data electronically? The world's contact management gurus long ago came up with a standard file format for contact data: the vCard. It's a kind of digital business card that exists as a separate file. People can pass this data along by attaching their (or someone else's) card to an email message.

If you get a message with contact data, you see an icon for the VCF file, as shown in Figure 8.8. To get this data into your Contacts list, follow these steps:

1. **In the Home screen, tap Mail to open the Mail app.**

2. **Tap the message that contains the vCard attachment.**

3. **Tap the icon for the vCard file.** Mail opens the vCard, as shown in Figure 8.8.

4. **Tap Create New Contact.** If the person is already in your Contacts list but the vCard contains new data, tap Add to Existing Contact and then tap the contact.

8.8 If your iPad receives an email message with an attached vCard, an icon for the file appears in the message body.

Sending and receiving a contact via AirDrop

Sharing your contact data using a vCard has worked well for many years, but sharing data via attachments is beginning to feel decidedly old-fashioned. Fortunately, these days of exchanging virtual business cards may soon be over thanks to a feature called AirDrop, which is a Bluetooth service that lets two nearby devices — specifically, any recent iPhone, iPad, or Mac — swap contacts directly. Here are the steps to follow:

1. **Use Contacts to open the contact you want to share.**

2. **Tap Share Contact.** The Share sheet appears.

3. **Tap AirDrop.** The AirDrop dialog opens and displays an icon for each nearby device.

4. **Tap the icon for the person or device with whom you want to share the contact.** The other person sees a dialog asking for permission to accept the contact. When she taps Accept, her version of Contacts loads and displays the contact.

Sorting contacts

By default, Contacts displays your contacts sorted by last name (or company name, for businesses) and then by first name (to resolve cases where people have the same last name). That makes sense in most cases, but you might prefer a friendlier approach that sorts contacts by first name and then by last name. Follow these steps to make it so:

1. **Open the Settings app.**

2. **Tap Contacts.** The Contacts settings appear.

3. **Tap Sort Order.** The Sort Order settings appear.

4. **Tap First, Last.** Contacts now sorts your contacts by first name.

Syncing contacts

Most of us spend a fair amount of time maintaining our contacts by adding, editing, and removing contacts and performing sundry other contact-related chores. The goal is a nicely curated list that's complete and up to date. Once you achieve that goal (or get close to it), the thought of repeating everything on your other devices (your iPhone, your Mac or PC, and so on) is unappealing, to say the least.

Forget that. Instead, if you have an iCloud account, you can configure that account to sync your contacts, which means not only that all your contacts appear on all your iCloud devices, but any changes you make to your contacts on any device will propagate to each device.

To make sure your iPad is syncing contacts, follow these steps:

1. **Open the Settings app.**

2. **Tap your name near the top of the Settings pane.** The Apple ID screen appears.

3. **Tap iCloud.** The Cloud settings appear.

4. **Make sure the Contacts switch is On.** Contacts now syncs your contacts with your iCloud devices.

Do you, like the White Rabbit in Lewis Carroll's *Alice's Adventures in Wonderland*, find yourself constantly saying, "Oh, my ears and whiskers, how late it's getting"? Well, you've come to the right place, because the iPad can help. Not only can you can use it to read *Alice's Adventures in Wonderland* (that will just make you later than you already are, though), but you can also take advantage of the Calendar and Reminder apps. They turn your tablet into an electronic administrative assistant that stores your future events and appointments and reminds you when they're coming up. Oh, my ears and whiskers, how punctual you'll be!

Getting Started with the Calendar App

Your iPad comes with an app called Calendar that you can use to track upcoming happenings, such as appointments, birthdays, meetings, dinner dates, and so on. Calendar calls these items *events* and offers lots of useful tools for tracking, managing, and remembering the events of your life.

You need the Calendar app up and running for this chapter, so head for the Home screen and tap the Calendar icon. Figure 9.1 shows the Calendar app in portrait mode.

Calendars

Inbox

9.1 Your tablet's administrative assistant: the beautiful and talented Calendar app.

Genius

You don't have to see only your iCloud account calendars in the Calendar app. If you add a third-party account such as Google, Microsoft Exchange, or Outlook.com to your iPad (see Chapter 5), you can view that account's calendars, as well. Open Settings, tap Mail, tap Accounts, tap the third-party account, and then tap the Calendars switch to On.

The key to getting around in the Calendar app efficiently is to take advantage of its various views, represented by the following four buttons at the top of the screen:

● **Day.** Shows the events of a single day. To navigate this view, tap a date near the top of the screen. To see more dates, scroll the displayed dates left or right.

● **Week.** Shows all your events for the selected week. To navigate this view, scroll the screen left or right.

Genius

In many countries (including the United States), Week view defaults to showing Sunday as the first day of the week. If that doesn't work for you, you can designate Monday (or any day you prefer) to be the start of the week. Open Settings, tap Calendar, tap Start Week On, and then tap the day you want to use as the start of your week.

● **Month.** Shows the titles of all your events for a given month. You navigate this view by scrolling up or down.

● **Year.** Shows a full calendar year. The dates on which you have scheduled events appear with a colored background. You navigate this view by scrolling up or down.

Genius

Month view shows just the title of each event, along with a color-coded bullet that tells you in which calendar the event resides. To see more details for an event, tap it. Calendar displays info such as the event's time, location, notes, and attendees.

Tracking Your Events

You never know when someone will invite you to lunch or to a get-together. Happily, if you have your trusty iPad at your side, you can check your schedule and add and edit events directly in the Calendar app. The next few sections provide the details.

Adding an event to your calendar

Follow these steps to add a basic event (I cover the more advanced features, such as repeating events and alerts, a bit later in this chapter):

1. **Display the date on which the event occurs.**

2. **Long press the time when the event occurs.**
   In Month view, long press the date. You can also tap New Event (+) near the top of the screen (to the left of the Day button). The New Event screen appears, as shown in Figure 9.2.

3. **Use the Title box to enter a title for the event.**

4. **(Optional) Use the Location box to select a location for the event.**

5. **Tap Starts and then set the time and date when your event begins.** If you're creating your event in Month view, you need to tap the All-Day switch to Off before you can set a start time for the event. I show you how to create all-day events later in this chapter.

6. **Tap Ends and then set the time and date when your event finishes.**

Cancel	New Event	Add
Title		
Location		
All-day		
Starts	Nov 9, 2020	12:00 PM
Ends		1:00 PM
Repeat		Never >
Travel Time		None >
Calendar		• Personal >
Invitees		None >
Alert		None >

9.2 Fill in the New Event dialog to add an event to your calendar.

7. **If you have two or more calendars, tap Calendar and then tap the calendar you want to use for this event.**

8. **(Optional) Use the Notes box (you need to scroll to the bottom of the New Event screen to see it) to enter your notes for the event.**

9. **Tap Add.** Calendar adds the new event to your calendar.

Editing an event

According to Murphy's Law of Calendars, after you add an event to your schedule, something about the event will inevitably change: the start time, the end time, the location, or perhaps all three. That's fine with you because Calendar makes it easy to edit the event and keep your schedule accurate.

Genius

If you just want to change the start or end time (or both), switch to either Day or Week view. Then, long press the event until Calendar adds selection handles to it. Drag the top selection handle to change the start time; drag the bottom selection handle to change the end time; drag any other part of the event to move it to a new time.

Follow these steps to edit an event:

1. **Display the date that contains the event you want to edit.** In Day view, navigate to the date. In Week or Month view, open the week or month that contains the date.

2. **Tap the event.**

3. **Tap Edit.** Calendar displays the event data in the Edit screen.

4. **Make your changes.**

5. **Tap Done.** Calendar saves your work and returns you to the event details.

Repeating an event

Lots of events are one-offs: They come, they go, and you move on with your life. However, you probably also schedule many different types of events that recur on a regular schedule: annual birthdays and anniversaries, a monthly departmental meeting at work, a weekly running club or book club. You might think these would be a hassle because they require you to put in regular work scheduling them, but that's not the case. Why not? Because Calendar comes with a Repeat feature where, given an event that recurs multiple times, you add only the next event and then ask Calendar to automatically repeat the event at the required recurrence interval (monthly, weekly, every 10 days, or whatever). You can configure the event to either repeat indefinitely or stop on a particular date.

Here are the steps to follow to repeat an existing event:

1. **Display the date that contains the event you want to edit.** In Day view, navigate to the date. In Week or Month view, open the week or month that contains the date.

2. **Tap the event.** Calendar opens the event info.

3. **Tap Edit.** Calendar displays the event data in the Edit screen.

4. **Tap Repeat.** The Repeat list appears.

5. **Tap the repeat interval you want to use.**

6. **Tap End Repeat.** The End Repeat list appears.

7. **You have the following two choices:**

   - **On Date.** Tap to have the event repeat only up to the date you specify.

   - **Never.** Tap to have the event repeat indefinitely.

8. **Tap Back (<).** Calendar returns you to the Edit Event screen.

9. **Tap Done.** Calendar repeats the event.

Converting an event to an all-day event

Consider the following list of event types:

- Birthday

- Anniversary

- Trade show

- Sales meeting

- Conference

- Vacation

What do all these types have in common? Their "duration" is effectively all day. A birthday or an anniversary is literally an all-day event, a vacation is (usually) a multiday event, and a work-related event such as a trade show or sales meeting usually lasts the whole workday.

Why is this important? Well, suppose you schedule a trade show as a regular event that lasts from 9 a.m. to 5 p.m. When you examine that day in the Calendar app Day or Week view, you see a big fat block that covers the entire day. If you also want to schedule meetings that occur at the trade show, Calendar lets you do that, but it shows these new events on top of this existing trade show event. This makes the schedule hard to read, so you might miss an event.

To solve this problem, configure the trade show (or whatever) as an all-day event. Calendar removes the event from the regular schedule and displays it separately, near the top of the Day view or on the top part of the Week view. That leaves the regular schedule free for other events. Follow these steps to configure an event as an all-day event:

1. **Display the date that contains the event you want to edit.** In Day view, navigate to the date. In Week or Month view, open the week or month that contains the date.

2. **Tap the event.** Calendar opens the event info.

3. **Tap Edit.** Calendar switches to the Edit screen.

4. **Tap the All-day switch to the On position.**

5. **Tap Done.** The Calendar app saves the event, returns you to the calendar, and now shows the event as an all-day event, as shown in Figure 9.3.

9.3 All-day events appear in the all-day section, near the top of the Day and Week views.

Adding an alert to an event

There are dozens of "productivity" gurus out there who, in exchange for a hefty slice of your savings, will tell you their secrets to being a productive and stress-free member of society. Let me save you a ton of money by letting you in on the most important of these secrets: Get stuff out of your head and into some kind of form where it can't be forgotten.

The gurus offer elaborate systems for doing this, but when it comes to handling events, Calendar's Alert feature is all you need. That is, if you have an important event coming up, don't fret that you might miss it. Instead, add it to your schedule and then configure Calendar with an alert to let you know when the event is about to happen (which could be a minute, an hour, or a day before — whatever works for you). And alerts also appear in your iPad's Notification Center, so even if you miss the actual alert, you can still see the notification.

Follow these steps to set an alert for an event:

1. **Display the date that contains the event you want to edit.** In Day view, navigate to the date. In Week or Month view, open the week or month that contains the date.

2. **Tap the event.** Calendar opens the event info.

3. **Tap Edit.** Calendar displays the event data in the Edit screen.

4. **Tap Alert.** The Event Alert list appears. Figure 9.4 shows the Event Alert list for a regular event; the list that appears for an all-day event offers slightly different choices.

5. **Tap the number of minutes, hours, or days before the event you want to see the alert.** If you're editing an all-day event, you can set the alert for 9 a.m. on the day of the event, 9 a.m. the day before the event, 9 a.m. two days before the event, or a week before the event.

6. **To set up a backup alert, tap the Second Alert option.** Next, tap the number of minutes, hours, or days before the event you want to see the second alert.

7. **Tap Done.** The Calendar app saves your alert choices and returns you to the calendar.

‹ New Event	**Alert**
None	
At time of event	
5 minutes before	
10 minutes before	
15 minutes before	
30 minutes before	
1 hour before	
2 hours before	
1 day before	
2 days before	
1 week before	

9.4 Use the Event Alert screen to tell Calendar when to remind you about your event.

Genius

You can set a default alert time for different event types. Open the Settings app, tap Calendars, and then tap Default Alert Times. Tap the event type you want to configure (Birthdays, Events, or All-Day Events) and then tap the default alert time you want Calendar to use.

Note

Calendar displays a chime each time it displays an alert. If you find these sounds annoying, you can turn them off. Open the Settings app and then tap Sounds. Tap Calendar Alerts and then tap None.

Getting More Out of the Calendar App

The basic features of the Calendar app — multiple views, color-coded calendars, repeating events, all-day events, and event alerts — make it an indispensable time-management tool. But it has a few more tricks up its sleeve that you ought to know about, and these are covered in the rest of this chapter.

Setting the default calendar

If you have multiple calendars on the go, each time you create a new event the Calendar automatically chooses one of your calendars by default. It's no big whoop if every now and then you have to tap the Calendar setting and choose a different calendar. However, if you have to do this most of the time, it gets old in a hurry, particularly when I tell you there's something you can do about it. Follow these steps to configure the Calendar app to use a different default calendar:

1. **Open the Settings app.**

2. **Tap Calendar.** The Calendar settings appear.

3. **Tap Default Calendar.** The Default Calendar screen appears.

4. **Tap the calendar you prefer to use as the default.** The Calendar app now uses that calendar as the default for each new event.

Subscribing to a calendar

If you know someone who has published a calendar, you might want to keep track of it within the Calendar app. You can do that by subscribing to the published calendar. The Calendar app sets up the published calendar as a separate item, so you can easily switch between your own calendars and the published one.

To pull this off, you need to know the web address of the published calendar. This address usually takes the following form: *server.com/calendar.ics*. Here, *server.com* is the address of the calendar server, and *calendar.ics* is the name of the file, which is almost always an iCalendar format file with the extension .ics, preceded (usually) by a folder location.

For calendars published to iCloud, the address always looks like this: *ical.icloud. com/member/calendar.ics*. Here, *member* is the iCloud member name of the person who published the calendar. Here's an example address: ical.icloud.com/aardvarksorenstam/aardvark.ics.

Follow these steps to subscribe to a published calendar:

1. **Open the Settings app.**

2. **Tap Calendar.** The Calendar settings appear.

3. **Tap Account.** The Account screen opens.

4. **Tap Add Account.** The Add Account screen opens.

5. **Tap Other.** The Settings app displays the Other screen.

159

6. **Tap Add Subscribed Calendar.** You see the Subscription dialog.

7. **Use the Server text box to type the calendar address.**

8. **Tap Next.** The Settings app connects to the calendar.

9. **Tap Save.** The Settings app adds an account for the subscribed calendar.

To view the subscribed calendar, open the Calendar app, click Calendars (pointed out earlier in Figure 9.1) to open the Calendars pane, and then tap to select the check box beside the subscribed calendar.

Controlling events with Siri voice commands

The Siri personal assistant offers a number of voice commands for creating, editing, and querying your events. To get Siri to schedule an event, you use the following general syntax: *Schedule what* with *whom* at *when*.

Here, *schedule* can be any of the following: "schedule," "meet," "set up a meeting," "new appointment."

The *what* part of the command (which is optional) determines the topic of the event, so it could be something like "Lunch" or "Budget review" or "Dentist"; you can also precede this part with "about" (for example, "about expenses"). The *whom* part of the command specifies the person you're meeting with, if any, so it can be a contact name or a relationship (such as "My husband" or "Dad"). The *when* part of the command sets the time and date of the event; the time portion can be a specific time such as "3" (meaning 3 p.m.) or "8 a.m.", or "noon"; the date portion can be "today" or "tomorrow", a day in the current week (such as "Tuesday" or "Friday"), a relative day (such as "next Monday"), or a specific date (such as "August 23rd").

See the following examples:

- "Schedule lunch with Karen tomorrow at noon."
- "Meet with my sister Friday at 4."
- "Set up a meeting about budgeting next Tuesday at 10 a.m."
- "New appointment with Sarah Currid on March 15 at 2:30."

You can also use Siri to modify existing events. For example, you can change the event time by using the verbs "Reschedule" or "Move," as shown in the following examples:

- "Reschedule my meeting with Sarah Currid to 3:30."
- "Move my noon appointment to 1:30."

You can also use the verb "Add" to include another person in a meeting, or the verb "Cancel" to remove a meeting from your schedule, as shown in the following examples:

- "Add Charles Aster to the budgeting meeting."

- "Cancel my lunch with Karen."

Finally, you can query your events to see what's coming up, as shown in the following examples:

- "When is my next appointment?"

- "When is my meeting with Sarah Currid?"

- "What is on my calendar tomorrow?"

- "What does the rest of my day look like?"

Handling Microsoft Exchange meeting requests

If you've set up a Microsoft Exchange account in your iPad (see Chapter 5), there's a good chance you're using its push features. This means that the Exchange Server automatically sends incoming email messages to the Mail app, as well as new (or changed) contact and calendar data. If someone back at headquarters adds your name to a scheduled meeting, Exchange generates an automatic meeting request, which is an email message that tells you about the meeting and asks if you want to attend.

How will you know? The Home screen's Calendar icon shows a badge with the number of pending requests. Also, in the Calendar app toolbar, the Inbox icon (pointed out earlier in Figure 9.1) tells you how many meeting requests you have waiting for you.

Note If you don't see the Inbox tray icon, then you need to turn on syncing for your Exchange calendar. Open Settings, tap Mail, tap Accounts, and then tap your Exchange account. Tap the Calendars switch to the On position, and when your iPad asks what you want to do with the local calendars, tap Keep on My iPad.

It's best to handle such requests as soon as you can, so here's what you do:

1. **Tap Inbox (see Figure 9.1).** Calendar displays your pending meeting requests.

2. **Tap the meeting request.** Calendar displays the meeting details.

3. **Tap your response:**

- **Accept.** Tap this button to confirm that you can attend the meeting.

- **Maybe.** Tap this button if you're not sure and will decide later.

- **Decline.** Tap this button to confirm that you can't attend the meeting.

Working with Reminders

The Calendar app is an excellent tool for tracking appointments, meetings, and other events. By adding an alert to an event you get a digital tap on the shoulder to remind you when and where your presence is required.

However, our days are sprinkled with tasks that don't quite qualify as Calendar-level events: It might be making a phone call, starting the laundry, or turning on the oven. These are tasks that need to be done — and need to be done at a certain time — but it seems like too much to add them as Calendar events.

For such mini-events, you're better off using the Reminders app, which displays a notification to remind you when it's time to perform the task.

Creating a time reminder

Follow these steps to set up a reminder that alerts you at a specific time:

1. **On the Home screen, tap Reminders.** The Reminders app appears. If the app asks for permission to use your location, tap Allow While Using App. I talk about location-based reminders in the next section.

2. **On the left side of the screen, tap the list you want to use to store the reminder.**

3. **On the right side of the screen, tap New Reminder.** Reminders creates a new reminder.

4. **Type the reminder text.**

5. **To add details, tap the More Info icon (*i*).** The Details dialog appears, as shown in Figure 9.5.

6. **Tap the Date switch to On and then use the calendar that appears to set the date of the reminder.**

9.5 Use the Details dialog to set up your reminder.

7. **Tap the Time switch to On and then use the controls that appear to set the time of the reminder.**

Genius

You can leave the Time switch Off to create an *all-day* reminder that appears at 9 a.m. on the date you choose. To choose a different time for your all-day reminders, open Settings, tap Reminders, and then select a time in the All-Day Reminders section.

8. **Use the Priority setting to assign a priority to the reminder: None, Low, Medium, or High.**

9. **Use the Notes text box to add some background text or other information about the reminder.**

10. **Tap Done.**

Creating a location reminder

Another way to set a reminder is to use a location. The Reminders app then creates a kind of border — called a *geofence* — around that location. When your iPad crosses that geofence, the reminder notification appears. You get to choose if the reminder appears when you're arriving at the location or leaving it. Here are the steps to follow to set up a location reminder:

1. **On the left side of the Reminders screen, tap the list you want to use to store the reminder.**

2. **On the right side of the screen, tap New Reminder.** Reminders creates a new reminder.

3. **Type the reminder text and then tap the More Info icon (*i*).** The Details dialog appears.

4. **Tap the Location switch to On.**

5. **Tap Custom.** The Location dialog appears.

6. **Use the Search box to specify the address of the location you want to use and then tap the location when it appears in the search results.** Alternatively, you can tap Current Location to use your present whereabouts.

7. **To have the reminder appear when your iPad first comes within range of the location, tap Arriving.** If you prefer to see the reminder when your iPad goes out of range of the location, tap Leaving, instead.

8. **Tap Back (<).**

9. **Use the Priority setting to assign a priority to the reminder: None, Low, Medium, or High.**

10. **Use the Notes text box to add some background text or other information about the reminder.**

11. **Tap Done.**

Creating a new list and setting the default list

The Reminders app comes with three preset lists that you can use: Reminders, Home, and Work. The default is Reminders, but you can also select a different list if it's more suitable or if you want to keep your personal and business reminders separate. If none of these three prefab lists is exactly right for your needs, feel free to create your own list by following these steps:

1. **In the Reminders app, tap Add List.** If you have multiple reminders-compatible accounts on your tablet, tap the account you want to use. Reminders creates the new list.

2. **Type the name of your list.**

3. **Tap Done.** The Reminders app adds the list to the left pane.

The default list is the one that Reminders uses when you don't specify a particular list when you create a reminder. Follow these steps to set a particular list as the default:

1. **On the Home screen, tap Settings to launch the Settings app.**

2. **Tap Reminders.** The Reminders screen appears.

3. **Tap Default List.** The Default List screen appears.

4. **Tap the list you want to use as the default.**

Completing a reminder

When a reminder is complete, you don't want it lingering in the Reminders list (or whatever list it's in), cluttering the screen, and making it hard to look through your remaining reminders. To avoid that, once the reminder is done, tap the radio button beside it. This tells Reminders that the reminder is complete, and the next time you display the list, you won't see the reminder (although you can always tap More — the three dots in the upper right corner and then tap Show Completed to see your completed reminders).

Deleting a reminder

If you no longer need a reminder, it's a good idea to delete it to keep your reminder lists neat and tidy. To delete a reminder, follow these steps:

1. **In the Reminder app, tap the list that contains the reminder you want to delete.** Reminders displays the list's reminders.

2. **Swipe left on the reminder you want to delete.** Reminders displays a Delete button.

3. **Tap Delete.** Reminders deletes the reminder.

Setting reminders with Siri voice commands

You can also create reminders via voice using the Siri app. Time-based reminders use the following general syntax: Remind me to *action* at *when*. Here, *action* is the task you want to be reminded to perform, and *when* is the date and time you want to be reminded (as described earlier in the chapter when I discuss creating calendar events using Siri). See the following examples:

- "Remind me to call my wife at 5."

- "Remind me to pick up Greg at the airport tomorrow at noon."

- "Remind me to bring lunch."

Location-based reminders use the following general syntax: Remind me to *action* when I *location*. Again, *action* is the task you want to be reminded to perform; *location* is the place around which you want the geofence set up (including either "get to" or "leave," depending on whether you want to be reminded coming or going). Review the following examples:

- "Remind me to pick up milk when I leave here."

- "Remind me to call my husband when I get to La Guardia airport."

- "Remind me to call my sister when I get home."

- "Remind me to grab my sample case when I arrive at Acme Limited."

For the last of these, you can assume that "Acme Limited" is a company name defined (with an address) in your Contacts list.

How Can I Navigate My World with iPad?

Your iPad comes with a built-in hardware that can determine your current location. That means you can use your iPad as a remarkably accurate mapping tool that enables you to not only locate specific addresses or places on a map, but also get directions to those locations, whether you're driving, walking, or taking transit. Whether you're trying to get from A to B or you just want to know if you can get there from here, your iPad's location services and its powerful Maps app can help. This chapter tells you everything you need to know.

Working with Location Services

iPadOS comes with a set of software and hardware features that fall under the heading of *Location Services* that give apps access to location data. Here are some examples:

- The Camera app uses Location Services to embed your current location into each photo you take.

- When you add a location to an event, the Calendar app uses Location Services to map that location.

- When you add a physical address to a contact, the Contacts app uses Location Services to map that address.

- When you create a reminder based on a location, the Reminders app uses Location Services to set up a geofence around that location.

- The Maps app uses Location Services to map and give directions to specific locations.

As you can see, Location Services is incredibly useful. However, your location data — especially your present location — is sensitive, private information that should be controlled as much as possible. The next few sections show you how.

Genius

Your iPad determines your current location by using data from Bluetooth connections and Wi-Fi networks. If you have an iPad model with built-in cellular network hardware, your iPad also determines your location by using the cellular network and GNSS (Global Navigation Satellite System) devices, particularly GPS (Global Positioning System) satellites.

Controlling how apps access Location Services

When you launch an app that would like to use location data, you see a dialog similar to the one displayed in Figure 10.1. Here, the app is requesting permission to use the iPad's location tools to determine your location. Most of the time you see the following four options:

- **Precise.** Determines whether the app can use your exact location (to within about 10 meters, or about 30 feet) or just an approximate location (to within about 2 kilometers — about a mile and a quarter — in urban locations and to within about 10 kilometers — about 6 miles — in rural locations). Tap Precise to toggle this setting between On and Off.

- **Allow Once.** Allows the app to use your location just this time. The app will ask again the next time you run it.

- **Allow While Using App.** Allows the app to use your location, but only when you're actually using the app. When you switch to a different app, the previous app no longer has access to your location.

- **Don't Allow.** Prevents the app from using your location.

Note, however, that whichever permissions you give the app, you can always change your mind later. Here are the steps to follow to control how an app can access Location Services:

1. **Open the Settings app.**

2. **Tap Privacy.** The Privacy settings appear.

3. **Tap Location Services.** The Location Services settings appear, as shown in Figure 10.2.

4. **Tap the app you want to work with.**

5. **Tap one of the following:**

   - **Never.** Prevents the app from using your location.

   - **Ask Next Time.** Configures the app to ask for permission to use your location the next time you run the app.

   - **While Using the App.** Gives the app permission to use your location when you use the app.

   - **Always.** Gives the app permission to use your location even when you're not using the app. (Note that this setting is available only for certain apps.)

6. **If you don't want the app to use your exact location, tap the Precise Location switch to Off.**

Note that the Location Services screen uses the following three icons (see Figure 10.2) to indicate which apps are using Location Services and how they're using them:

- A gray Location Services icon tells you that the app has used your location in the previous 24 hours.

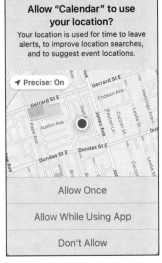

Allow "Calendar" to use your location?

Your location is used for time to leave alerts, to improve location searches, and to suggest event locations.

Allow Once

Allow While Using App

Don't Allow

10.1 Apps that can use location data require your permission to use that data.

App has used your location in the past 24 hours

10.2 Use the Location Services settings to control how apps can access your location.

- A solid purple Location Services icon tells you that the app has recently used your location.

- An outlined purple Location Services icon tells you the app has set up a geofence around your location.

The active Location Services status also appears in the status bar, to the left of the battery status.

Shutting off Location Services

Instead of denying access to Location Services app by app, there might be times when you want to deny *all* apps access to your location:

● You're going to a private location, and you want to be sure that no app is tracking you.

● Your iPad battery is getting low. Location Services tend to use up battery power, so turning off these features can preserve battery life.

Whatever the reason, follow these steps to shut off Location Services for all apps:

1. **Open the Settings app.**

2. **Tap Privacy.** The Privacy settings appear.

3. **Tap Location Services.** The Location Services settings appear.

4. **Tap the Location Services switch to Off.** If you have Find My iPad activated, Settings asks you to confirm.

5. **Tap Turn Off.** Settings shuts off app access to Location Services.

Mapping Locations

Lots of apps can take advantage of your iPad's Location Services, but arguably the most important of these is the Maps app, which you can use to locate specific addresses or places on a digital map and, as I describe later, to get turn-by-turn directions to a location.

Tap the Maps icon in the Home screen and the initial Maps screen appears, as shown in Figure 10.3. (If you see a dialog letting you know that Maps would like to use your current location, say "But of course!" and tap Allow While Using App.)

Searching for a location

The most straightforward way to view a location in Maps is to search for the location using an address, name, or some other text. Follow these steps to search for a location:

1. **Tap in the Search for a Place or Address box in the upper left corner of the screen.**

2. **Type some text that specifies the location you want.** You can enter any of the following:

   ● The name of the location.

   ● The address of the location.

   ● A word or phrase that describes the location.

   As you type, Maps displays a list of locations that match.

10.3 Use the Maps app to map your world.

3. **Tap the location you want in the search results.** Maps displays the destination on the map and displays an information card with data about the location, as shown in Figure 10.4.

The information card that Maps displays offers a wealth of data (depending on how public the location is), including the phone number, street address, hours of operation, photos, website address, and more. The info also ties into Yelp, a service that offers user-generated content — particularly ratings, reviews, and photos — of millions of locations around the world.

Genius

If you have a Yelp account, you can add your own content about the destination. In the What People Say section, tap Open Yelp to launch the Yelp app.

Information card

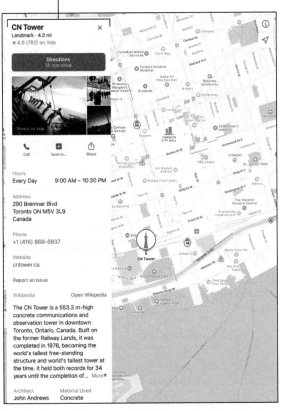

10.4 When you tap a location in the search results, Maps displays the location on the map and displays an information card for the location.

Marking a location

Searching for a location works if you happen to know the location's address or name. However, sometimes you just know approximately where you want to go, without knowing an address, a place name, and any other information that would help with a Maps search.

That's not a problem because Maps supports a special feature called a *marked location*, which is a pushpin added to the map on any spot that you long press. Maps also displays the Marked Location information card, which includes the address of the location, its latitude and longitude, and the name of any business (such as a shop or restaurant) that happens to be at the address.

Flying over your destination

When someone says she's getting *a bird's-eye view*, she's speaking metaphorically about seeing an overview of something. With the Maps app, however, that phrase comes about as close to being literal as you can get without actually jumping into a plane or helicopter (or somehow transforming yourself into a bird). That's because Maps comes with a feature called Flyover that gives you an interactive, three-dimensional aerial view of a destination. What use is that? Well, not much, I suppose, but it *is* jaw-dropping.

Follow these steps to enable Flyover for a destination:

1. **Search for the destination to get its location on-screen.**

2. **If the location's information card includes a Flyover button, tap that button and skip the rest of these steps.**

3. **Tap the More (i) icon in upper right corner of the Maps screen.** The Maps Settings dialog appears.

4. **Tap Satellite.** Maps switches from Standard view to Satellite view.

5. **Tap 3D.** Maps enables Flyover mode. Figure 10.5 shows Maps in Flyover mode featuring Toronto's CN Tower. Flyover mode is best for tall buildings and structures; it's not much good for street-level views.

Once you have Flyover on the go, you can use the following techniques to interactively fly around your destination:

- Spread two fingers to zoom in or pinch two fingers to zoom out.
- Swipe down to fly past the destination and swipe up to fly back.
- Swipe right to pan to the left and swipe left to pan to the right.
- Rotate two fingers (clockwise or counterclockwise) to fly in a circle.
- Simultaneously spread two fingers and slide up to reduce elevation; simultaneously pinch two fingers and slide down to increase elevation.

Mapping your current location

Many parks, malls, and other venues offer maps to help you get the lay of the land. Most of the time, these maps have a "You Are Here" marker that points out the location of the map (and, hence, *you*), which is a great way to get your bearings in unfamiliar territory.

10.5 Bird's-eye view, indeed; Maps in Flyover mode.

If you've ever found yourself walking around a new city or an unfamiliar part of town, you might yearn for some kind of "You Are Here" marker to suddenly appear. Well, your iPad can do that! The Maps app offers a Tracking icon (see Figure 10.6) that, when tapped, will show you the exact location of your iPad (and, hence, *you*).

Your tablet examines Wi-Fi hotspots and (if your iPad is cellular-equipped) GPS coordinates and nearby cellular towers to figure out your current position. When the necessary triangulating is complete, Maps zooms in on your current area and displays a blue dot that represents your location, as shown in Figure 10.6. Tap the Tracking icon a second time and Maps orients the map to face in the same direction as your iPad and also rotates the map along with your iPad.

Tracking icon

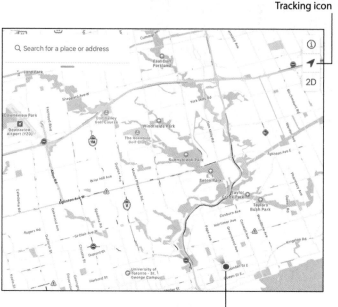

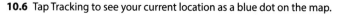

Current location

10.6 Tap Tracking to see your current location as a blue dot on the map.

Genius

Knowing where you are is a good thing, but it's even better to know what's nearby. Suppose you're in a new city and you're dying for a cup of coffee. Tap in the Search box, type **coffee** and then tap Search. Maps drops a bunch of pins on nearby locations that match your search. Tap a pin to see an information card that includes the location's phone number, address, and website.

Mapping a contact's address

If you've used the Contacts app to add a street address to a contact, you can display that address on a map by following these steps:

1. **Open the Contacts app.**

2. **Tap the contact that you want to map.** The Contacts app displays that person's data.

3. **Tap the address that you want to view.** Your iPad switches to Maps and drops a pin on the contact's address.

Genius

The opposite (sort of) technique would be to map an address and then add that address to one of your contacts. To do this, search for the address you want to use. In the location's information card, tap Add to Existing Contact and then tap the contact in the list that appears.

Mapping an address from an email

If you receive an email message that includes a street address (say, as part of the sender's signature), you might want to know where that address is located. You could copy the address from the message and then paste it into the Search for a Place or Address text box in Maps, but there's no need to go to that much trouble. Instead, you can follow these much easier steps:

1. **In the Mail app, display the message that includes the address.** If your tablet is in portrait mode, tap Inbox to see the messages.

2. **Long press the address in the message to display a list of actions.** If the address is displayed as a link (that is, underlined in a blue font), it means Mail has recognized it as an address, so you can just tap the address and skip the next step.

3. **Tap Open in Maps.** Maps opens and drops a pin on the address.

Saving a location as a favorite

If you know the address of the location you want to map, you can add a pushpin for that location by opening Maps and running a search on the address. That is, you tap the Search box in the menu bar, type the address, and then tap the Search button.

That's no big deal for one-time-only searches, but what about a location you refer to frequently? Typing that address over and over gets old in a hurry, I assure you. You can save time and tapping by telling Maps to save that location on its Favorites list, which means you can access it, usually, with just a few taps.

Use either of the following techniques to add a location to the Favorites list:

⊚ Map the location you want to save and then tap Add to Favorites in the location's information card.

⊚ In the Favorites section that appears under the Search for a Place or Address text box, tap Add, search for the location you want to add, tap it in the search results, use the Details pane to name the favorite, and then tap Done.

To map a favorite location, follow these steps:

1. **Tap inside the Search box.**

2. **If you don't see the favorite you want, tap See All.** Maps displays the Favorites pane.

3. **Tap the location you want to map.** Maps displays the appropriate map and adds a pin for the location.

Sharing a map

To send someone a map via email, text message, AirDrop, or some other sharing method, follow these steps:

1. **Map the location you want to send.**

2. **In the location's information card, tap Share.** Maps displays a list of ways to share the map.

3. **Tap the method you want to use to share the map.**

4. **If the method is text-based (such as an email or text), fill in the rest of your message and send it.**

Mapping locations with Siri voice commands

You can use the Siri voice-activated assistant to control Maps with straightforward voice commands. You can display a location, get directions, and even display traffic information. Press and hold the Top button (if your iPad supports Face ID) or the Home button (for all other iPad models) until Siri appears.

To display a location in Maps via Siri, say "Show *location*" (or "Map *location*" or "Find *location*" or "Where is *location*"), where *location* is an address, a name, or a Maps favorite. Similarly, to get directions from Siri, say "Directions to *location*," where *location* is an address, a name, or a Maps favorite. To see the current traffic conditions, say "Traffic *location*," where *location* can be a specific place or somewhere local, such as "around here" or "nearby." To get your current location, you can say "Where am I?" or "Show my current location."

Navigating with Maps

One possible navigation scenario with Maps is to specify a destination (using a contact, an address search, a marked location, or a favorite) and then tap the Tracking icon. This gives you a map that shows both your destination and your current location. Depending on how far away the destination is, you may need to zoom out (by pinching the screen or tapping it with two fingers) to see both locations on the map. You can then eyeball the streets to see how to get from here to there.

Eyeball the streets? Hah, how primitive! Maps can bring you into the twenty-first century not only by showing you a route to the destination, but also by providing you with the distance and time it should take and by giving you street-by-street, turn-by-turn instructions, whether you're driving or walking. It's one of the sweetest Maps features, and the next few sections provide the details.

Getting directions to a location

Here are the basic steps to follow to get directions to a location:

1. **Use Maps to add a pushpin for your destination.** Use whatever method works best for you: the Contacts list, an address search, a marked location, or a favorite.

2. **Tap Directions in the location's information card.** Maps displays several possible routes, as shown in Figure 10.7.

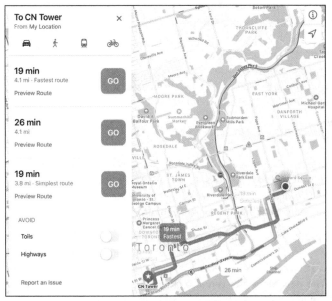

10.7 Maps offers a few driving routes originating from your current location.

3. **To use a different starting point, follow these substeps:**

   a. **Tap My Location.** Maps opens the Change Route dialog, shown in Figure 10.8.

   b. **Select or enter a new location in the From box.**

   c. **Tap Route.** Maps returns you to the routes.

Genius

If you need directions *from* the destination rather than *to* it, display the Change Route dialog and then tap Swap (pointed out in Figure 10.8). Maps swaps the locations.

4. **Tap the icon for the type of directions you want: Drive, Walk, Transit, or Bicycle.**

5. **Tap the Go button for the route you want to take.** Maps displays the first leg of the journey.

Maps features turn-by-turn directions. This means that as you approach each turn, Siri tells you what to do next, such as "In 400 feet, turn right onto Main Street." Maps also follows along the route, so you can see where you're

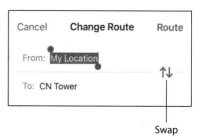

10.8 Use the Change Route dialog to specify a different starting location.

going and which turn is coming up. You can see your estimated time of arrival, remaining travel time, and distance remaining by tapping the screen.

Getting live traffic information

Okay, it's pretty darn amazing that your iPad can tell you precisely where you are and how to get somewhere else. However, in most cities, it's the getting somewhere else part that's the problem. Why? One word: traffic. Maps may tell you the trip should take 10 minutes, but that could easily turn into a half-hour or more if you run into a traffic jam.

That's life in the big city, right? Maybe not. If you're on a highway in a major North American city, Maps can most likely supply you with — wait for it — real-time traffic conditions. This is really an amazing tool that can help you avoid traffic messes and find alternative routes to your destination. The new Maps app can also show you traffic construction spots, and it gathers real-time information from Maps users to generate even more accurate traffic data. If you're in the middle of turn-by-turn directions, Maps will even recognize an upcoming traffic delay and offer an alternative route around it!

To see the traffic data, tap More (i) in the upper right corner of the screen and then tap the Traffic switch to On. Maps displays an orange line to indicate traffic slowdowns, a red line to indicate very heavy traffic, and Roadwork icons to indicate construction sites. Tap a Roadwork icon to see more information about the work, as shown in Figure 10.9.

10.9 Tap a Roadwork icon to see info about the construction.

Getting directions with Siri voice commands

You can also use Siri to get directions and display traffic information. Tap and hold the Top button (if your iPad supports Face ID) or the Home button (for all other iPad models) until Siri appears.

To get directions from Siri, say "Directions to *location*," where *location* is an address, a name, or a Maps favorite. To see the current traffic conditions, say "Traffic *location*," where *location* can be a specific place or somewhere local, such as "around here" or "nearby."

How Do I Protect My iPad?

Your iPad is a tablet, but that humble word doesn't begin to do it justice. After all, you can use your iPad as a camera, a video recorder, a scheduler, an address book, a map, a notepad, a media player, a virtual assistant, a messenger, a web browser, and much more. This remarkable versatility also means your iPad is stuffed with a huge amount of your personal data. Although you might not store any state secrets on your device, chances are that what you *do* store there is important. Therefore, it makes sense to take a few minutes now to configure your iPad so that your data is protected should your tablet get lost or fall into the wrong hands. This chapter shows you what you need to do.

Locking Your iPad

When your iPad displays its Lock screen, the device is locked in the sense that tapping the touchscreen or pressing the volume controls does nothing. This arrangement prevents accidental taps on something significant when the device is rattling around in your backpack or handbag. To unlock the device once you have the Lock screen displayed, you use one of the following techniques:

- **Your iPad supports Face ID.** Swipe up from the bottom of the screen.

- **All other iPads.** Press the Home button.

Note | If you have a cover for your iPad — such as the Apple Smart Cover or Smart Folio — you can also unlock or lock your tablet by opening or closing the cover. If you find that you frequently remove the cover without wanting to unlock your iPad, you can turn off the automatic lock. Tap Settings, tap Display & Brightness, and then tap the Lock/Unlock switch to Off.

Simple, right? Yes, unfortunately so. Why? Because the ease with which you can unlock your iPad means that anyone else who gets his mitts on your tablet can unlock it just as easily. If you have sensitive or private information on your device — particularly if you've set up Apple Pay with one or more credit cards (see Chapter 3) — you need to truly lock your iPad. The next few sections show you how to lock your tablet using a passcode, as well as with Touch ID or Face ID.

Locking your iPad with a passcode

No matter what model of iPad you use, your first line of defense is to set up a passcode that must be typed before iPadOS will display the Home screen. You can set either a simple four-digit passcode or a longer, more complex one that uses any combination of numbers, letters, and symbols.

Here are the steps to follow to lock your iPad with a passcode:

1. **Open the Settings app.**

2. **Tap one of the following:**

    - **If your iPad supports Face ID.** Tap Face ID & Passcode.

    - **For all other iPad models.** Tap Touch ID & Passcode.

3. **Tap Turn Passcode On.** The Set Passcode dialog appears.

4. **To use something other than the default six-digit passcode, tap Passcode Options and then tap the passcode type you prefer.**

5. **Type your passcode and, if you're entering a complex passcode, tap Next.** Settings asks you to reenter your passcode.

6. **Type your passcode again and, if you're typing a complex passcode, tap Done.** If iPadOS prompts you for your Apple ID password, type your password and then tap Sign In.

Caution

Please don't forget your passcode! If you do, iPadOS will lock you out of your own device. You can still get back in, but the only route is a drastic one: Restore the tablet's data and settings from an existing backup (which I describe in Chapter 12).

With your passcode now active, Settings enables the passcode-related settings in the Face ID & Passcode (or Touch ID & Passcode) screen, as shown in Figure 11.1. You can also get to this screen by opening Settings, tapping Face ID & Passcode (or Touch ID & Passcode), and then typing your passcode.

This screen offers the following options:

- **Turn Passcode Off.** If you want to stop using your passcode, tap this button and then type the passcode (for security; otherwise, an interloper could just shut off the passcode).

- **Change Passcode.** Tap this button to type a new passcode. Note that you first need to type your old passcode and then type the new one.

- **Require Passcode.** This setting determines how much time elapses before the tablet locks the device and requests the passcode. You can choose from the following options:

  - The default setting is Immediately, which means you see the Enter Passcode screen as soon as you attempt to unlock your iPad.

  - The other options are After 1 minute, After 5 minutes, After 15 minutes, and After 1 hour. Use one of these if you want to be able to work with your tablet for a bit before getting locked out. For example, the After 1 minute option is good if you need to quickly check email without having to type your passcode.

- **Allow Access When Locked.** This section displays an On/Off switch for each feature you can use when your tablet is locked, such as Today View, Notification Center,

Control Center, and Siri. When any of these settings are On, you can use the associated feature even when your iPad is locked. For example, if the Siri switch is On, you can search the web and perform other voice-related tasks from the Lock screen. If you change any of these settings to Off, you can no longer use the associated feature when your tablet is locked.

- **Erase Data.** If you turn this setting On, your iPad erases all its data after ten consecutive incorrect passcode attempts. That many passcode failures is a sure sign that someone is trying to break into your iPad by guessing the passcode. If your iPad contains extremely sensitive or private information, you probably don't want to take the chance that the person might guess the correct passcode, so it's a good idea to activate this setting and have the data erased automatically.

With the passcode activated, when you bring the iPad out of standby and attempt to unlock the screen (by swiping up from the bottom of the screen or by pressing the Home button), the Enter Passcode screen appears (see Figure 11.2). Type your passcode (and tap Done if it's a complex passcode) to unlock the tablet.

Face ID & Passcode
Set Up Face ID
ATTENTION
Require Attention for Face ID
TrueDepth camera will provide an additional level of security by verifying that you are looking at iPad before unlocking. Some sunglasses may block attention detection.
Attention Aware Features
iPad will check for attention before dimming the display, expanding a notification when locked, or lowering the volume of some alerts.
Turn Passcode Off
Change Passcode
Require Passcode   Immediately >
ALLOW ACCESS WHEN LOCKED:
Today View
Notification Center
Control Center
Siri
Home Control
Return Missed Calls
USB Accessories
Unlock iPad to allow USB accessories to connect when it has been more than an hour since your iPad was locked.
Erase Data
Erase all data on this iPad after 10 failed passcode attempts.
Data protection is enabled.

11.1 Use the passcode-related settings to configure the passcode lock.

Locking your iPad with a fingerprint

If you have an iPad, iPad Air, or iPad mini, you can protect your tablet using Touch ID, the fingerprint sensor built into either the Home button (iPad and iPad mini) or the Top switch (iPad Air). By teaching the device your unique fingerprint, you can unlock your tablet merely by leaving your finger or thumb resting on the fingerprint sensor. You can use the same fingerprint to approve purchases you make in the iTunes Store, the App Store, and retailers that accept Apple Pay. Here's how to set up Touch ID:

1. **Open the Settings app.**

2. **Tap Touch ID & Passcode and then type your passcode (if you have one) to open the Touch ID & Passcode screen.**

Note If you haven't set up a passcode, Settings will require you to enter one after you finish adding your first fingerprint. Therefore, you might as well set up a passcode now; see the previous section for the instructions.

3. **Tap Add a Fingerprint.** The Touch ID screen appears.

4. **Lightly rest your thumb — or whatever finger you most often use when you're unlocking your iPad — on the fingerprint sensor.** Again, remember that the location of the fingerprint sensor depends on your iPad model:

   • **iPad or iPad mini.** The fingerprint sensor is part of the Home button.

   • **iPad Air.** The fingerprint sensor is built into the Top switch.

5. **Repeatedly lift and place your finger as Touch ID learns your fingerprint pattern.**

6. **When you see the Adjust Your Grip screen, tap Continue.**

7. **Once again, repeatedly lift and place your finger, this time emphasizing the edges of the finger.**

11.2 This is the screen you see when using a complex passcode to unlock your iPad.

8. **When you see the Complete screen, tap Continue.**

9. **To specify another fingerprint, repeat Steps 3 to 8.**

Here's how you use Touch ID:

• **Unlock your iPad.** Using a fingerprint-scanned finger, press and hold either the Home button (iPad or iPad mini) or the Top switch (iPad Air) until the Home screen appears.

• **Make an iTunes purchase.** In the iTunes Store or the App Store, tap the price of the item you want to buy and then tap the Buy button. When the Touch ID dialog appears, rest your finger on the Home button (iPad or iPad mini) or the Top switch (iPad Air) until the purchase is approved.

● **Make an in-app purchase.** For apps that support Apple Pay, tap the Apple Pay button in the checkout screen and then place your scanned finger over the Home button (iPad or iPad mini) or the Top switch (iPad Air).

● **Make an Apple Pay purchase.** You can use Touch ID to pay for goods in the real world without having to use cash or a credit card. In a merchant that accepts Apple Pay, place your scanned finger over the Home button (iPad or iPad mini) or the Top switch (iPad Air) and then hold the tablet near the store's contactless reader.

Locking your iPad with facial recognition

Recent versions of the iPad Pro — that is, all generations of the 11-inch iPad Pro and the third generation and later of the 12.9-inch iPad Pro — replace Touch ID with Face ID, which enables you to unlock your tablet using facial recognition. By letting your iPad learn to recognize your face, you can unlock the device just by looking at it. This works even if you're wearing sunglasses, have a hat on, or haven't shaved for a few days.

Note

Face ID does *not* work if you're wearing a mask, such as the cloth masks so many of us used to get through the COVID-19 pandemic.

You can also use facial recognition to approve purchases you make via the iTunes Store, the App Store, and Apple Pay, as well as authorize the use of AutoFill passwords.

Here are the steps to follow to configure Face ID:

1. **Open the Settings app.**

2. **Tap Face ID & Passcode and then type your passcode (if you have one) to open the Face ID & Passcode screen.**

Note

No passcode? That's fine, but note that Settings will require you to enter one after you finish scanning your face, so you might as well set up a passcode now as I describe earlier in this chapter.

3. **Tap Set Up Face ID.** The How to Set Up Face ID screen appears.

4. **Tap Get Started.** Settings displays a frame on the screen.

5. **Position your face within the frame and then slowly rotate your head until you fill in the circle that appears.** When the circle is complete, the first Face ID scan is complete.

6. **Tap Continue.**

7. **Once again, position your face within the frame and then slowly rotate your head until you fill in the circle that appears.** When the circle is complete, the second Face ID scan is complete.

8. **Tap Done.**

With your face scan complete, you can start using Face ID. In the Face ID & Passcode screen (see Figure 11.3), you see the following four switches in the Use Face ID For section:

- **iPad Unlock.** When this switch is On, you unlock your iPad by waking it and then looking directly at the screen. When the lock icon at the top of the screen unlocks, you can swipe up from the bottom of the screen to continue.

- **iTunes & App Store.** When this switch is On, you can use your face to authorize a purchase in the iTunes Store or the App Store.

- **Apple Pay.** When this switch is On, you can use your face to authorize Apple Pay purchases.

- **Password AutoFill.** When this switch is On, you can use your face to fill in saved login credentials.

11.3 Use these Face ID switches to control what you can authorize with your face.

Configuring Your Tablet to Sleep Automatically

You can put your iPad into Standby mode at any time by tapping the Top button once. This drops the power consumption considerably (mostly because it shuts off the screen), but you can still receive incoming notifications and text messages. Also, if you have the Music app running, it continues to play.

However, if your tablet is on but you're not using it, the device automatically goes into Standby mode after two minutes. This is called Auto-Lock, and it's a handy feature because it saves battery power and prevents accidental taps when your iPad is just sitting there.

It's also a crucial feature if you've protected your tablet with a passcode lock, Touch ID, or Face ID, as I describe earlier, because if your device never sleeps, it never locks either unless you shut it off manually.

To make sure that your iPad sleeps automatically or if you're not comfortable with the default two-minute Auto-Lock interval, you can make it shorter, make it longer, or turn it off altogether. Follow these steps to do so:

1. **Open the Settings app.**

2. **Tap Display & Brightness.** The Display & Brightness settings appear.

3. **Tap Auto-Lock.** The Auto-Lock screen appears.

4. **Tap the interval that you want to use.** You have five choices: 2 Minutes, 5 Minutes, 10 Minutes, 15 Minutes, or Never.

Backing Up Your Tablet

The data you have on your iPad might not be vital in the overall scheme of things, but there's no doubt it's vitally important to *you*. Therefore, it makes sense to protect your tablet's data and settings by backing up your iPad to your iCloud account. That way, if you lose your tablet or you have to erase it because of a problem, you can at least restore your data and settings from the backup (I should you how this is done in Chapter 12).

Follow these steps to back up your iPad's data and settings to iCloud:

1. **Open the Settings app.**

2. **Tap your name near the top of the Settings pane.** The Apple ID settings appear.

3. **Tap iCloud.**

4. **Tap iCloud Backup.**

5. **Check that the iCloud Backup switch is On**, as shown in Figure 11.4. If not, tap the switch to On. This configures iPadOS to make automatic backups whenever it is locked, connected to a Wi-Fi network, and plugged in to a power source.

6. **Tap Back Up Now.** iPadOS backs up your tablet's data to your iCloud account.

11.4 Make sure the iCloud Backup switch is On for automatic iPad backups.

Setting Restrictions on a Child's iPad

If you have a child with an iPad, there are some tasks you probably don't want that child to perform on the tablet: installing apps, changing settings, making in-app purchases, and so on.

If your children have access to your iPad, you probably don't want them installing or deleting apps or editing your account settings. Similarly, if they have tablets of their own, you may be a bit worried about some of the content they might be exposed to on the web, on YouTube, or in iTunes. You also might not want them giving away their current location.

For all those and similar parental worries, you can sleep better at night by activating the parental controls. Follow these steps to set these controls, and restrict the content and activities that kids can see and do:

1. **Open the Settings app on your child's iPad.**

2. **Tap Screen Time.** The first time you tap Screen Time, you see an overview of the feature, so tap Continue to move on. Screen Time asks whether this is your iPad or your child's.

191

3. **Tap This is My Child's iPad.** The Downtime dialog appears. You use Downtime to set times when the child can't use the iPad without your permission.

4. **Use the Start and End controls to set a schedule for when the child isn't allowed to use the tablet; when you're done, tap Set Downtime.** The App Limits dialog appears. You use App Limits to set the maximum time the child is allowed to use certain app categories, such as Games.

5. **Select the check box beside each app category you want to limit (alternatively, select the All Apps & Categories check box to set a limit on everything at once); in the Time Amount setting, tap Set and then select the maximum number of hours and/or minutes the child is allowed for the selected app categories; then tap Set App Limit.** The Content & Privacy settings appear.

6. **This screen is just an overview, so tap Continue.** (To actually set these restrictions, complete these steps and then tap Content & Privacy Restrictions in the Screen Time settings.) iPadOS asks you to enter a Screen Time passcode. You use this passcode to access the Screen Time settings and to override the restrictions you've set.

Note

The Screen Time passcode is not the same as the passcode you use to unlock your iPad.

7. **Type the passcode you want to use; then type the passcode again when prompted.** iPadOS prompts you to enter Apple ID credentials, which you can use to reset your Screen Time passcode if you forget it.

8. **Enter your Apple ID email address and password and then tap OK.**

How Do I Solve iPad Problems?

Your iPad's exterior is simple — it's really nothing more than a chunk of glass with a metal backing and hardly any moving parts — but the interior tells a completely different story: This is one fancy device that's stuffed with chips, sensors, transceivers, and other electronic bric-a-brac. Your iPad is, in short, a full-blown computer that — given its lightning-fast processor, heaps of memory, and large solid-state storage — can perform some pretty amazing tricks. That's the good news. The bad news is that every computer ever made eventually has problems, which means there's a good chance that someday your iPad will behave strangely or just stop working. When that day comes, this chapter gives you a step-by-step guide to troubleshooting whatever problem you're having.

Troubleshooting iPad Problems: A Quick Guide

If your iPad starts acting weirdly, it's tempting to leap to the conclusion that the device itself is broken in some way. That's not impossible, but your iPad's innards have no moving parts, so it's very unlikely that some internal component has gone south. Instead, you can solve the vast majority of iPad woes by following this general ten-step troubleshooting procedure:

1. **Shut down whatever app you're using.**

2. **If you recently changed a setting, restore the setting to its previous state.**

3. **Shut down and restart your iPad.**

4. **Reboot your iPad's hardware.**

5. **Recharge your iPad.**

6. **Check for and install iPadOS updates.**

7. **Free up some storage space on your iPad.**

8. **Check your Wi-Fi network connection.**

9. **Reset any settings that are related to the problem you're having (such as resetting network settings if you're having connection issues).**

10. **Erase your iPad and restore a backup.**

Note

To be clear, you don't have to run through all 10 steps for every problem. Start with Step 1 and, if that doesn't solve the glitch, proceed to Step 2. Continue working through the steps until you've solved the problem, and then move on to bigger and better things.

Troubleshooting iPad Problems Step-by-Step

The next few sections take you through each of the troubleshooting steps from the previous section in a bit more detail.

Step 1: Shut down whatever app you're using

If your iPad is unresponsive, it usually means that the app you're using has crashed and has taken your iPad down with it. Most of the time, you can get your iPad going again by forcing the stuck app to quit. Here are the steps to follow:

1. **Display the multitasking screen:**

   - **All iPad models.** Swipe up from the bottom of the screen; then pause when you reach the middle of the screen.

   - **iPad models with a Home button.** Double-press the Home button.

2. **Scroll right or left as needed to bring the app's thumbnail into view.**

3. **Drag the app thumbnail up to the top of the screen, as shown in Figure 12.1.** iPadOS sends the thumbnail off the screen and shuts down the app.

Caution

Lots of iPad users force-quit apps even when the apps are working fine. However, this is a sure-fire way to reduce your iPad's battery life because iPadOS has to spend extra battery power the next time you start any app that you force-quit. Unless an app is unresponsive, you should never have to force-quit any app you've used on your iPad.

If your iPad is unresponsive and you can't display the multitasking screen, you can follow these alternative steps if your iPad has a Home button:

1. **Press and hold the Top switch until you see the Slide to Power Off screen; then release the Top switch.**

2. **Press and hold the Home button for about six seconds.** Your iPad shuts down the current app and returns you to the Home screen.

Note

If your unresponsive iPad doesn't have a Home button, then you need to restart your iPad, as I describe a bit later in this chapter.

197

Drag the app thumbnail up to the top of the screen

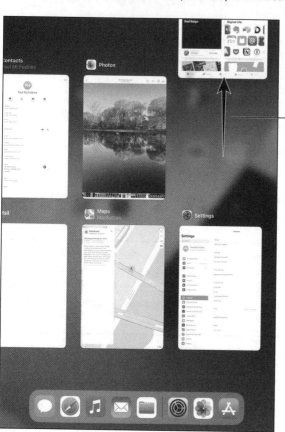

12.1 To force-quit a frozen app, drag its multitasking screen thumbnail up to the top of the screen.

Step 2: Restore a changed setting

If you make a change in the Settings app and your iPad immediately starts behaving erratically, then there's a strong chance the changed setting is the culprit. If you can still get to the Settings app, open it and restore the setting to its previous state. If your iPad is unresponsive, restart it (see the next section) and then revert the change in Settings.

Step 3: Shut down and then restart your iPad

If your iPad is frozen, you won't be able to access either the multitasking screen or the Settings app — in fact, you won't be able to do anything at all with your iPad. Anything, that is, except shut down your iPad and then restart it. What good does that do? It reloads iPadOS — your iPad's operating system software — which almost always solves whatever glitch was causing your tablet to go haywire.

How you begin the shutdown procedure depends on which iPad model you're using:

- **iPads without a Home button.** Hold down both the Top switch and one of the volume buttons until you see the Slide to Power Off slider, as shown in Figure 12.2.

- **iPads with a Home button.** Press and hold the Top switch until you see the Slide to Power Off slider.

Press and hold the Top switch and a volume button

12.2 On iPads without a Home button, press and hold the Top switch and a volume button.

Either way, drag the Slide to Power Off slider to the right to start the shutdown. Give the device a few seconds to turn everything off. To restart, press and hold the Top switch and then release the switch when you see the Apple logo.

Step 4: Reboot the iPad hardware

Restarting iPadOS, as I describe in the previous section, is usually enough to solve any iPad problem, but not always. If either the problem still exists after the iPadOS restart or your iPad won't shut down at all, then your next step is to reboot the tablet hardware.

How you do a hardware reboot depends on your iPad model:

- **iPads without a Home button.** Press and release the Volume Up button; press and release the Volume Down button; press and hold down the Top switch until you see the Apple logo.

- **iPads with a Home button.** Press and hold the Top switch and the Home button until you see the Apple logo.

Step 5: Recharge your iPad

If your iPad is unresponsive and won't turn on at all, the most likely culprit is that the battery is completely out of juice. Connect your tablet to a power outlet and wait for a while. If after a minute or two the device turns on and you see the battery logo, then you know the tablet is charging and will be back up and running in a few minutes.

Step 6: Check for iPadOS updates

Many iPad problems are caused by errors — known in programming parlance as *bugs* — in iPadOS or some other piece of your iPad's system software. There's a good chance Apple knows (or will soon know) about the glitch, will (eventually) fix it, and will then make the fix available as part of an iPadOS update.

You can check for and install iPadOS updates by following these steps:

1. **Open the Settings app.**

2. **Tap General.** Settings displays the General screen.

3. **Tap Software Update.** Settings begins checking for available updates. If you see the message "Your software is up to date," then you can move on to bigger and better things.

4. **If an update is available, tap Download and Install.** Settings downloads the update and then proceeds with the installation, which takes a few minutes.

Caution

Your tablet will only go through with the update if it has more than 50 percent battery life through the entire update operation. To ensure the update is a success, either plug your tablet into an AC outlet or only run the update when the battery is fully charged.

Step 7: Free up storage space

Your iPad uses its internal storage space to hold many things, including iPadOS, the apps that come preinstalled on your iPad as well as the apps you install, the content you create with those apps, and so on. However, your iPad also uses its internal storage as a kind of temporary work area. If the iPad's memory space gets full, iPadOS will offload some of the contents of memory to its internal storage to make room in memory for new apps or content.

All this happens automatically and *way* behind the scenes, so you never have to worry about any of it. Or, I should say, you never have to worry about any of it *until* your iPad's internal storage is nearly full and it becomes more difficult for iPadOS to manage memory and perform certain operations. When that happens, you start seeing error messages letting you know that some operation can't be completed because there is "No space left on device" or "There is not enough available storage." You might also see a message like the one shown in Figure 12.3.

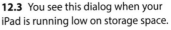

iPad Storage Full
You can free up space on this iPad by managing your storage in Settings.

Not Now | Settings

12.3 You see this dialog when your iPad is running low on storage space.

If you see any of these low-storage messages, you need to free up some storage space on your iPad pronto. Fortunately, iPadOS gives you several different ways to free up some space. To see these methods, use either of the following techniques to display the iPad Storage settings:

- If you have the message shown in Figure 12.3 on-screen, tap Settings.
- Open the Settings app, tap General and then tap iPad Storage.

Either way, you end up at the iPad Storage screen, shown in Figure 12.4. The chart at the top of the screen shows how much of your iPad's storage space is used and how much of that space is used by various categories of data, such as Apps, System (that is, iPadOS), and Photos.

You also usually see a Recommendations section that offers one or more suggestions for saving storage space. You should try these recommendations before trying anything else.

Next, take a look at the list of apps to see which ones are taking up the most storage space. Chances are you'll see one or more apps that are taking up an unreasonable amount of space. If so, you can take back some or all of that space using any of the following techniques:

- **Offload the app.** Tap the app, tap Offload App, and then tap Offload App when iPadOS asks for confirmation. This method removes the app from your iPad but keeps the app's data. Use this method for large apps that aren't storing tons of data on your iPad.

- **Delete the app.** Tap the app, tap Delete App, and then tap Delete App when iPadOS asks you to confirm. Use this method for apps that are storing a lot of data on your iPad (assuming you no longer need that data). Note that this method is not available for many of the apps that come preinstalled on your iPad (such as Photos and iCloud Drive).

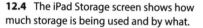

| ‹ General | iPad Storage | Q |

iPad — 31.4 GB of 32 GB Used

● Apps ● System ● Photos ● Messages ● Media ● Other

RECOMMENDATIONS

Offload Unused Apps — Enable

Automatically offload unused apps when you're low on storage. Your documents & data will be saved.

Review Large Attachments — ›

Save up to 150.8 MB - See photos, videos, and attachments taking up storage in Messages and consider deleting them.

iMovie — 775.4 MB ›
Last Used: 11/5/20

Photos — 616.3 MB ›
Last Used: Yesterday

Globe2Go — 554.5 MB ›
Last Used: Today

Numbers — 477.2 MB ›

Keynote — 471.3 MB ›

12.4 The iPad Storage screen shows how much storage is being used and by what.

- **Delete some or all of the app's data.** Tap the app to display its data usage. If you see a Documents section, such as the one shown in Figure 12.5 for the Messages app, tap a document category, and then tap Edit to put the category in edit mode. Tap to select the check box beside each item you want to delete and then tap Delete (the trashcan icon).

Step 8: Check your Wi-Fi connection

Some apps either will stop working or will act erratically if they lose access to the Internet. So if an app is acting weird — or if you can't do any Internet-related chores such as view websites or check email — it could be that your iPad's Wi-Fi connection is missing in action.

Genius

If you have an iPad that supports cellular connections and you're out of range of a Wi-Fi network, you might have problems with any app that isn't configured to use cellular data. To fix this, open Settings, tap Cellular, locate the app in the Cellular Data section, and then tap the app's switch to On.

Checking Wi-Fi means performing two separate troubleshooting steps: Check your iPad's Wi-Fi connection and check your router's connection to the Internet.

On your iPad, here are a few things to go through:

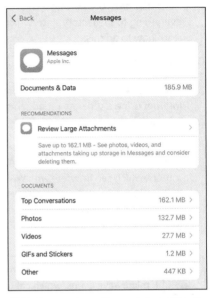

12.5 If an app has a Documents section, it means you can free up storage space by deleting individual data items from the app.

- **Check that the Wi-Fi antenna is turned on.** Open the Settings app, tap Wi-Fi, and then, if necessary, tap the Wi-Fi switch to On.

- **Check how far your iPad is from your router.** A lack of Wi-Fi could mean your tablet is too far from the router. For most routers, the maximum range is about 230 feet.

- **Check that Airplane Mode is turned Off.** Open Settings and then, if necessary, tap the Airplane Mode switch to Off. Alternatively, display the Control Center and then tap to turn off the Airplane Mode icon.

- **Check that your iPad is still connected to your W-Fi network.** Open Settings and check the Wi-Fi setting. If you see Not Connected, tap Wi-Fi, and then tap your network to reconnect.

- **Renew the Wi-Fi connection lease.** When your iPad connects to a Wi-Fi network, the router gives the tablet a *lease*, which is a kind of permission to access the network. You can sometimes solve a connectivity issue by renewing your iPad's lease. Open the Settings app, tap Wi-Fi, and then tap the More Info (*i*) icon to the right of the connected network. Tap Renew Lease, and when Settings ask you to confirm, tap Renew Lease.

- **Disconnect from and then reconnect to the network.** Open Settings, tap Wi-Fi, and then tap the More Info (*i*) icon to the right of the connected network. Tap Forget This Network to disconnect from the network and discard the network's saved login credentials. Tap your network and enter the password to reconnect.

- **Restart your iPad.** See the previous Step 3.

- **Reset the network settings.** This removes all stored network data and resets everything to the factory state, which might solve the problem. See Step 9, next, to learn how to do this.

On your Wi-Fi router, try these troubleshooting ideas:

- **Turn your Wi-Fi router off and then on again.** If your network accesses the Internet using a separate broadband modem, turn the modem off then on again, as well.

- **Check for interference.** Many household devices — such as baby monitors and cordless phones — use the same 2.4 GHz radio frequency (RF) band as most Wi-Fi routers, which can interfere with Wi-Fi signals. If you have such a device near your Wi-Fi router, either turn off the device or move it away from the router. Alternatively, set up a new Wi-Fi network using the 5 GHz band, if your router supports this (see your router documentation).

Caution

You should keep your tablet and wireless access point well away from microwave ovens, which can jam wireless signals.

- **Update the router firmware.** *Firmware* refers to the internal system software that runs the router. Router companies routinely offer firmware updates that fix device problems, so updating the router firmware might solve whatever connectivity issues you're having (see your router documentation).

- **Restore the router's factory settings.** If the router's settings are corrupted, you can reset the device to its original factory settings (see the router documentation). If you go this route, once the reset is complete, you'll need to set up your network again from scratch.

Step 9: Reset your settings

A common cause of iPad wonkiness is when one or more of the tablet's settings gets corrupted. For example, if you can't connect to a known Wi-Fi network, it might mean that your iPad's network settings are broken. You can almost always work around such problems by resetting some or all of your iPad's settings. Here are the steps to follow:

1. **Open the Settings app.**

2. **Tap General.**

3. **Tap Reset.**

4. **You have two choices:**

   - **Reset a specific type of setting.** Tap the corresponding Reset button. For example, if you're having connection troubles, tap Reset Network Settings.

   - **Reset every setting.** Tap Reset All Settings.

   Settings prompts you for your passcode.

5. **Type your passcode.** Settings asks you to confirm that you want to perform the reset.

6. **Tap Reset.**

Step 10: Erase and restore your content and settings

If you have a backup of your iPad (I talk about creating iPad backups in Chapter 11), then you can solve even the most recalcitrant problems by completely erasing all your iPad's settings and content and starting over with a fresh system. You can then restore your backup and you're back in business.

Here are the steps to follow to erase your settings and contents and restore from a backup:

1. **Open the Settings app.**

2. **Tap General.**

3. **Tap Reset.**

4. **Tap Erase All Content and Settings.** Settings asks if you want to update your iPad's iCloud backup before continuing.

5. **If you have a recent backup already in iCloud, tap Erase Now.** Otherwise, tap Backup Then Erase. Settings prompts you for your passcode.

6. **Type your passcode.** Settings asks you to confirm that you want to erase your iPad.

7. **Tap Erase.** Settings once again asks if you're sure you want to erase your iPad.

8. **Tap Erase.** iPadOS asks you to enter your Apple ID password.

9. **Type your password and then tap Erase.** iPadOS erases your iPad and then restarts a few minutes later.

10. **Run through the startup steps: selecting a language, country, and so on.** If you're prompted to choose how you want to restore your iPad, tap Other Options. Eventually you see the App & Data dialog.

11. **Tap Restore from iCloud Backup.** The Choose Backup dialog appears.

12. **Tap your most recent iPad backup.**

13. **Continue with the rest of the setup steps.** You eventually see the Restore from iCloud screen, which shows the progress of the restore. After a few minutes, your iPad reboots, and you see your restored content and settings.

Note

iPadOS at first restores only enough to get you back up and running. The full restore from iCloud can take quite a long time, so in the interim you might find that some content, apps, or other features are temporarily unavailable.

Index